CREATE SPACE FOR PEACE

forty years of peacemaking

GENE STOLTZFUS

1940-2010

Profits from the sales of this book will go to
Christian Peacemaker Teams (CPT)

Christian Peacemaker Teams place violence reduction teams in situations of crisis and occupation and militarized areas around the world at the invitation of local peace and human rights workers. They enlist the whole church in an organized non-violent alternative to war.

visit: http://cpt.org/

Join us at the following sites:

www.createspaceforpeace.info
www.facebook.com/spaceforpeace
Twitter:@space4peace
www.peaceprobe.wordpress.com

CREATE SPACE
FOR PEACE

Edited by

Dorothy Friesen

Marilen Abesamis

A PUBLICATION OF TriMark Press, Inc.
368 S. Military Trail • Deerfield Beach, FL 33442 • 800-889-0693
WWW.TRIMARKPRESS.COM

REQUEST FOR PERMISSION TO MAKE COPIES OF ANY PART OF THE WORK SHOULD BE
MAILED TO THE FOLLOWING ADDRESS: PERMISSION DEPARTMENT,
TRIMARK PRESS, INC., 368 SOUTH MILITARY TRAIL, DEERFIELD BEACH, FLORIDA 33442
800-889-0693 / WWW.TRIMARKPRESS.COM

LIBRARY OF CONGRESS CATALOGING-IN-PUBLICATIONS DATA IS AVAILABLE
FRIESEN, DOROTHY
CREATE SPACE FOR PEACE, GENE STOLTZFUS

ISBN: 978-0-9829702-4-9
A11, FIRST EDITION
PRINTED IN THE UNITED STATES

TO ORDER COPIES OF THIS PUBLICATION VISIT:
WWW.CREATESPACEFORPEACE.INFO
WWW.TRIMARKPRESS.COM

A PUBLICATION OF TRIMARK PRESS, INC.
368 S. MILITARY TRAIL • DEERFIELD BEACH, FL 33442 • 800-889-0693
WWW.TRIMARKPRESS.COM

TABLE OF CONTENTS

Gene was such a strong presence in everything he did.
He lived his life as a truly Human One.
Our heartfelt thanks for his life.

– June and Walter Wink, Sandisfield, Massachusetts March, 2010

ACKNOWLEDGMENTS

Our hearts are filled with gratitude for the team of people who loved Gene and generously contributed their time and skills to make this book a reality in time for the first anniversary of his death.

Madeleine Enns and Harold Neufeld in Winnipeg cheerfully shouldered much of the work of copy editing and, as it turned out, proof reading as well. They also offered a shoulder to lean on and a house to stay at when needed. Photo Editor, Dale Fast in Chicago, made an invaluable contribution with his smooth, efficient, and professional response to our every request. Our digital guru, Wilson Tan in Singapore, led the way with an energetic and well thought-out plan for publicity. It was a joy to work with this team.

We thank Anne Stewart in Ely, who graciously opened her house for us to edit there, and then also worked with the manuscript. Karen Dannenmann and Claire Evans gave helpful feedback on specific portions of the book. Christian Peacemaker Team staff and International Voluntary Services, (IVS) alumni contributed photos or helped identify them. Elizabeth Hickman of TriMark Press was wonderful to work with. Special thanks to Phil Stoltzfus, Gene's nephew, who started the ball rolling by compiling Gene's writing and speeches.

INTRODUCTION

Gene Stolzfus, a full time activist and administrator in both church related and peace and justice organizations for over forty years, consistently put his body on the line for peace and helped others do the same. But he rarely wrote about it.

Most of the material in this book is taken from speeches and sermons, letters and his weekly blog reflections written between 2005 and 2010 after he retired as the founding director of Christian Peacemaker Teams. This collection does not explore Gene's entire biography nor feature all his writings and speeches. That kind of extensive compilation is for another type of book. The purpose of *Create Space for Peace* is to offer a flavor of Gene's life and work that can serve to inspire all of us to live and love our lives more fully.

Gene believed the world desperately needs peacemakers who engage nonviolently from a confident spiritual core, informed by critical thinking. In the introduction to his blog, *peaceprobe.wordpress.com*, he wrote, "All such work will affect the body politic, and will lead through periods of resistance to change. At root, all of us in this world have the potential to share the power of love, a force that reaches far beyond sentimentality."

The ideas about unarmed peacemaking work took organizational shape through Christian Peacemaker Teams (CPT). At Gene's memorial service in Goshen, Indiana, current Co-director, Doug Pritchard, summarized the work of CPT this way: "Over the years Gene and CPT reached out in life and death to communities around the world including urban peacemaking work in Washington DC and Richmond, Virginia; a peace delegation to Iraq on the eve of the Gulf War in 1991; Haiti, during the bloody years of the US backed coup that overthrew democratically elected President Jean Bertrand Aristide; Palestine/Israel, beginning around the second Intifada in 1995; supporting the struggles of First Nations communities throughout North America in relation to land and resources, including Lakota in South Dakota, Anishinaabek in Ontario, Oneida in New York, Miq'mak in New Brunswick; Chiapas, Mexico, around the Acteal massacre of 1997; Colombia, accompanying communities displaced by paramilitary and US-funded government violence and fumigation; Iraq, prior to the US invasion in 2003 and throughout the occupation; and the Pakistan/Afghan border region shortly after 9/11 and again in 2009. In death and in life, we carry forward the vision."

For Gene, everything connected to everything else and so, in a single blog entry, he effortlessly blended dreams, foreign policy, childhood experiences, and political investigation spanning several countries. No matter how we tried to arrange the material, each piece escaped and managed to intertwine with pieces in other sections to reflect the whole. The flow of the book is not chronological, but each article is dated, and to aid the reader we supply a chronology of Gene's life.

Part I: Shine the Light shows how early influences and choices Gene made as a young man are reflected in the actions he took in later years. *Part II: Circling the Globe*, draws from Gene's experiences around the world and demonstrates how he connected what he saw to his responsibility as a US citizen. *Part III: The Practice of Peacemaking* contains stories of direct peace actions as well as practical advice for peacemakers, including current political and military trends to address. *Part IV: A Life Well Lived* features a few last reflections by Gene, and then summarizes his contributions in the words of several colleagues and family members. The *Addendum* is a representative collection of poignant reflections and remembrances from Gene's friends and co-workers through the years.

We suggest approaching *Create Space* in the spirit of walking a labyrinth. On the labyrinth's winding path we may feel we are circling the outer edges, and then sense we are almost at the center before the path meanders toward the far periphery that actually brings us closer to the core of the story Gene lived. And we remember a labyrinth is not a maze; there are no dead ends. The consistent thread leading us through side trips into fantasy, sociological analysis, or emotional archetypes reflects Gene's deep sense that the way out of our global morass is to build a culture of peace that goes beyond knee jerk obeisance to settling conflict and righting injustices through violence and force.

Gene sends us in smaller and larger circles toward the sacred core and, just as mysteriously, circles us back to the entrance where we face ourselves and our choices in this world. We can then realize as Gene did, the blessing is in the journey itself.

A memorial stone for Gene is at this peace labyrinth at the Sacred Grove in Wisconsin, home of long-time friends Pat and Lucy Basler

PART I

SHINE THE LIGHT

We begin the labyrinth walk of Create Space for Peace at a time of crisis for Christian Peace Maker Teams (CPT) and Gene. As Dr. Martin Luther King Jr. has said, the ultimate measure of a person is where he stands in times of challenge and controversy. Though Gene had already retired as founding director of Christian Peacemaker Teams (CPT), the winter of 2006 was one of the bleakest moments for anyone connected in any way to CPT. Four CPT'ers taken by gun point in Baghdad in late 2005 were still being held incommunicado with no solid lead regarding their whereabouts or hope of release. The first item in this section is Gene's sermon delivered at that time. As it turned out, Harmeet Singh Sooden, New Zealand, Norman Kember, U.K. and Jim Loney, Canada were held until March 23, 2006. CPT was informed on March 10, 2006 that the body of Tom Fox, the only American among the hostages, was found in Baghdad.

Part I highlights Gene's participation in the campaign to Shine the Light on Washington, DC during the hostage crisis and introduces some earlier influences that led him to take this initiative, namely his grass roots experience in Vietnam 1963-67 during the US military build-up, his years of lobbying in Washington 1967-72, and his religious formation within a family deeply rooted in the Anabaptist peace tradition.

SHINE THE LIGHT

Sermon at Hyattsville Mennonite Church
January 24, 2006

I am in Washington today to join others in an effort to Shine the Light on the institutional sources of violence and terrorism in our nation. Every day at 3:00 p.m. we will walk around one of the places where violence is imagined or supported and then walk to the White House where we will pray. We invite you to join us. As we begin this witness I wish I could promise you that violence and terror will vanish forever, that our Christian Peacemakers Team (CPT) colleagues and all detainees will be released, and abuse will forever be vanquished. In fact I can't promise you anything, not one positive result. Some sincerely believe that we will make things worse. Others sincerely believe that by choosing the language of Light we reflect an arrogance that may lead to further conflict. Many think we are just one more eccentric, misguided and irrelevant, maybe fanatical expression of Christian faith. Our message may be misinterpreted, maligned, or distorted in the media.

As we begin this Shine the Light experience we do so as imperfect and often wounded people. But we are also people who have grown through our wounds and the pain of abuse that we have witnessed around the world. We have learned that light is more powerful than its absence. We have learned that the great forces of the world are frightened by the light. But every time we have to begin again, with our doubts, our unfinished confidence and our prayer that God's will can be done on earth. Great threads of hope are being given to us today by the world wide church, by the Muslim world, and by our own culture which is yearning to rid itself of violence.

In the years I was with CPT, our teams tried to begin the day with common worship. I am sure our primitive attempts at worship must have looked wimpy to our Muslim friends whose ritual of five prayer periods every day was so clear, and confident. I noticed over the years that when life got more dangerous and severe, prayer time for Muslims became more disciplined. I also noticed that when we felt threatened, demeaned, or desperate to break through the silence of oppression with an act of love, our own worship which included scripture, songs, and prayer became more focused. Sometimes, in our confusion, laughter would lace our prayers. Other times someone might jump up in the middle of our serious gathering seized by the Spirit with a message or a song. Some of us doubted the messenger but we knew we might just as well start listening to the Spirit.

Worship times launched us into discussions of the day's activities. The internal silence that could stymie us was broken and the real discussion about the oppressive outside silence could begin. What to do? Ideas tumbled out and organizers in the team listened for the patterns in the chaotic threads. They searched for a way to weave them into a tapestry for action and witness, a cloth that would draw attention to the horror that the team was witnessing but with a luminous streak of hope which the darkness could not dim. When I was with CPT that was the way it worked some days when things were down.

> **Muslim Peacemaker Teams**
> Appalled by the violence conducted in the name of Islam around the world, a group of Muslims, including human rights lawyers, wanted to promote non-violence in a way similar to CPT but grounded in Islam's tenets. In 2005 CPT conducted training in Karbala for the first Muslim Peacemaker Team (MPT). CPT and MPT worked together to clean up rubble left by US attacks in Fallujah. Only two months before CPTers were taken hostage, the two groups accompanied Palestinian Iraqis fleeing the country.

Two years ago I was in Baghdad where I spoke with many Muslim leaders in the mosques. For some it may have been their first contact with Christians. We listened to each other explain our work and our needs. Some understood that Christians thought of all of them as terrorists. Many were outraged by the disappearances of people in their community and the residual effect of the occupation, which to them was terrorism. We were also concerned about these matters and found common ground. When we described our work in nonviolence and our refusal to accept armed protection or rescue even when detained, they listened and said, "That is what Islam is about." Other leaders said, "It wouldn't work here." I saw them open themselves to the power of peace based on fairness in the Muslim tradition. The fact that so many Muslim leaders have spoken up on behalf of detainees, including CPTers, is not an accident. This speaking up is a way to counteract the hijacking of faith by states and groups working out of the energy of pain and retribution.

On 9/11 I watched as the towers of finance and industry burned. I thought this was an opportunity to put our best agape love-inspired imaginations to work. The world felt broken. Why would God allow this, unless it was a reminder to us of our deepest task as Christians. When the CPTers were detained in Baghdad, I was again reminded of how our agape love-inspired imaginations were presented with another opportunity.

Terrorists of all kinds—guerrilla supported, organized crime and state supported—believe that their pains will be made right by killing an enemy. By lashing back we set the terms for still another generation of terror. Our culture has worked this way for more than 5000 years back to the days of city states in Iraq. Despite the weight of this cultural tradition our hearts are gladdened when we read the great outpouring of public criticism of the war in Iraq. During the Vietnam war it took us years to reach this point. In the space of less than three years we have reached a critical point where our government must acknowledge the great chorus for peace.

God did not create us to be instruments of violent retribution. God created us as peacemakers, instruments of light and salt, and people of sacrifice and prayer. The program of the Prince of Peace did not include repaying evil for evil. Jesus proposed a program of enemy loving. I don't presume to know the full dimensions of that program but I have enjoyed many occasions when

I saw it work. The Prince's program suggested a complete paradigm shift in how violence is engaged. We live in a time when experiments to carry out this new paradigm are widely initiated—conflict resolution, nonviolent communication, nonviolent direct action—all of which have some roots in the stories of the Prince before he was killed by the State.

As we consider the great congregation of believers, we are captivated by the legacy of pain, abuse, and brokenness passed from generation to generation—some would say "Unto the seventh generation." I call upon us to awaken the souls of broken warriors, so hungry for hope, so ready to know the fullness of the Prince's program of peace, so wanting to believe.

What a blessing this century can be when Christians come together in a renaissance of peacemaking, harmonized and completed by the diverse gifts of nationality, culture, and gender. There is power in the people of faith to make all things new. I believe we have been placed here for a time like this to reinvigorate humanity's journey. This is the time to be pastors to all God's family.

The termination of terror, torture, and war is not up to Washington. Or Baghdad. Or Kabul. Or London. Or Tokyo. Or Delhi. Or Paris. Or Jerusalem. It is up to us. As we pray together we will find ways to take on more responsibility for the power that we have been given. The cost to us will not show up on our credit card. We have the power in our internal bank, the power of enemy loving. It has only one condition. If this power does not get used, it molds and smells bad; and the residue might create another disease. Prepare for surprises. This detainee crisis on the back of a generation of torture and terror has shaken the Muslim world into genuine steps of faithfulness, to the highest call within their tradition. I believe that Christians are feeling similarly called.

> I served in Mennonite Voluntary Service in Fort Wayne, Indiana, in the 1970s when Gene was executive director of the national program. He taught me that speaking out against injustice was Christian, a concept I never grasped from my evangelical childhood. To me, he represented the power of love and of telling the truth, even when difficult or dangerous. Gene was the most important mentor in my life. I am planning to teach an adult Sunday school class at my church, Portland Mennonite, using the essays from his blog. The truth never dies.
>
> - *Allan Classen, Portland, Oregon*

Twenty years ago, during the discussions about the founding of Christian Peacemaker Teams, I realized that despite so many voices to the contrary a sizable minority in our churches were joined by many other mainline and evangelical groups, and Roman Catholics representing a potent force for world peace. I believed that, if organized, we could fundamentally impact spiritual health, social structures, and the perceived legitimacy of war for nations and neighborhoods striving to achieve justice. The incredible power of active, nonviolent peacemaking is a premier sign of our time. People of faith have witnessed the effectiveness of nonviolence to push back violence and killing, often with amazingly small doses of organized action. We no longer need to be surprised by this.

The effectiveness of nonviolence has been adequately tested but we are in fact caught in a history that still waits for us to demonstrate this power fully. Over the last 20 years, I have carried on conversations about nonviolence and faith in more than 20 countries with people who are open to active nonviolence. But they believe that, until nonviolence is demonstrated more comprehensively, the threat of the gun must be maintained to keep their society secure. The final elimination of military force, armed police, and national and international guerilla action will be accomplished when a broader culture of nonviolence is expanded exponentially.

In an age when millions are anxious, and long for structures that bring peace, the sign of hope that a peace church can bring is breathtaking. Our work together up to this time has been preparation, pilot projects where our faith and confidence are tested and our skills refined. Forty years of peace work has taught me that our world is waiting for us to move beyond pilot projects to invite the Gospel of peace to become fully visible and for nonviolence to become a viable choice for every citizen. This can be the defining sign of the 21st century. "Where have you been all these years?" were the first words spoken to me during my visit to an Afghan leader some years ago.

This question reverberates in my soul every day as I try to pray.

How should we pray? Should we pray that our four friends be released? Should we pray that all detainees be released? Should we pray that God's will be done on earth as in heaven? Should we pray that the power of holy peacemaking will be revealed in its fullness?

At Cheap Street Church Hall, Sherborne, UK (2009)

Let us remember that in times of crisis . . .

- our understanding of life and death may be clarified and expanded,
- our lives may become more closely attuned with God's spirit for this, our age,
- in life and in death the highest good may be achieved through prayer and sacrifice,
- we can choose to be candles of light wherever long shadows stretch over hidden pain,
- the Glory of God will be revealed and all flesh and all creation will see that Glory together.

Vigil at the Pentagon
January, 2006

For ten days during January, 2006, vigils in Washington DC were held daily to Shine the Light on the various tentacles of war making—the Pentagon, the Department of Justice, Andrews Air Force Base, an Army Recruiting Station, the Federal Bureau of Investigation, the Internal Revenue Service which collects the money to support war, Homeland Security, the Capitol Building (House and Senate), the White House, the World Bank and International Monetary Fund, the Department of Veterans Affairs and Lockheed Martin, one of the world's mightiest defense contractors. Gene wrote about their daily experiences in his blog, peaceprobe.wordpress.com. Below is an excerpt from the Shine the Light series.

At the Pentagon Pat Basler, a member of our group with a hood over his head, is tethered by rope to another member simulating pictures of detainees in Iraq, Afghanistan, Guantanamo, and secret prisons that span the globe. We tell our entire story with one sign and the hooded one.

Our time is interrupted when the Pentagon Protective Service spokesperson repeatedly approaches to push us further and further from the masses of people passing by on the walk way. With a mixture of suggestions, humor, requests, and compliments I try to preserve space for our small circle. But by the time we take our leave, the Pentagon Protective Service, 25 men strong, has created a silent, empty area between us and the masses of this day's foot soldiers, hundreds of state supported employees passing by on their way from an office to a meeting, or to a shift change, all in the service of defending the country and making the world order come out right.

I notice the people who pass us look carefully at our sign but their eyes drop when they see the hooded one. What has the bent hooded one ignited in our common silence?

That empty security corridor has a sacred quality, an interim safe place where the Divine can remind us all, holy warriors and holy peacemakers, of the freedom and hope of the light. As I peer into that space I can see a new energy for our global civilization. This energy will help us reach beyond the smoke of the fuel that we burn, beyond the engines of power and destruction that we have all helped to create, to a moment in time when Love to which all creation is pulling us, begins to fill that space with music that we all can learn to sing.

Shine The Light Procession in Washington, DC (2006)

STEPPING INTO THE STREAM OF HISTORY

By Earl Martin

Gene Stoltzfus and I first met in Saigon in 1966. He had already been in Vietnam for three years with the International Voluntary Services (IVS). I was just arriving for a three-year assignment with the Mennonite Central Committee. That land of war would be the arena where both Gene and I would cut our political teeth. During those years, we heard the nightly shelling, we saw the daily bombing raids, we carried the bloodied bodies. In 1967 Gene decided, with other IVS personnel, to resign en masse to protest U.S. war policy. That act caught national attention.

Though Gene then returned to the US, his passion for ending the bloodshed in Vietnam continued strongly. For years he traveled across the country and in Washington DC telling the stories of the war and calling for a cessation of the war-making.

By early 1975, the US had withdrawn its combat troops from Vietnam, but thousands of American advisors and other officials remained in country. The US was funding 85% of the war which had now been "Vietnamized" with troops of the Saigon government. It appeared that the war could continue indefinitely, with unending American funding.

In January of 1975, our family was living in Quang Ngai, 500 miles north of Saigon, with the assignment of researching the problem of unexploded munitions left in the countryside after years of fighting. One day we received a telegram from the US saying, "Meet me in Saigon at the Continental Hotel on February 24 at 3 p.m." It was signed, "Proudfoot."

Neither Pat nor I could figure out who was sending this message. Yet there seemed to be an authenticity about it, and after discussing it, we decided that I should go to Saigon to check it out. When I arrived in Saigon, there was Gene! Had I known German, I might have been able to figure out that Stoltzfus translated as "Proudfoot"! Gene explained that a delegation of the U.S. Congress was coming to the country that night to review U.S. military spending in Vietnam. They would, of course, be hosted by the American Embassy, and would be introduced to the highest officials of the Saigon government regime. But Gene had contacted them in Washington before the trip to tell them that if they wanted to see more than what the Embassy would show them, he would try to arrange that for them.

That night, in the Embassy Guest House, we were sitting down with Bella Abzug (yes, with her big hats in Saigon!), Millicent Fenwick (yes, smoking her cigars!), Pete McCloskey and other congresspersons to plan encounters for them not only with the top government officials, but also with the victims of the war: the displaced refugee farmers, the Buddhist peace activists, the political prisoners who had gone through torture and grim years in prison.

As a result, when that delegation of American legislators went back to Washington, they were able to paint a picture to help the rest of Congress understand the true effects of American money going to the Saigon regime. Shortly thereafter, the Congress voted to cut off its limitless funding to the Saigon regime, and the war ended within several months.

With these bold acts of faith, Gene forged the way for many of us peace activists to believe that keen, strategic thinking and acting could not only "speak truth to power," but actually effect change in some of the government's most destructive policies.

Gene studied the movements of history and the unfolding of current events. Within that matrix, he would ask himself and his colleagues, "How can followers of Jesus step into that stream of history to bend its flow toward greater hope, more life and fairness for the folks caught in that stream?"

Gene Stoltzfus understood power like few others in the peace movement. He had seen the nature of empire, from a biblical perspective, as well as empire in its more current manifestations. He was relaxed in meeting with top government or military officials and was totally at home drinking tea with farmers in their local villages. Over the years, Gene had myriad contacts with high-level bureaucrats, but in the end he instinctively trusted the grassroots more than the powerful at the top. He saw power emanating most effectively from the bottom up.

And in all this, Gene was deeply Christian, or shall I say, deeply a follower of Jesus. While Gene worked intimately with Buddhist and Muslim partners over the years, it was always clear that Gene's own journey emanated from his radical commitment to Jesus' way of loving enemies and suffering love.

As director of the Christian Peacemaker Teams, Gene was always analyzing situations of conflict to discern where peacemakers might intervene in ways that would make the reality of conflict stunningly clear. Hence during the Iraq War, Gene visited Baghdad, consulted widely and then decided that CPT would help families find and contact their loved ones who were being held anonymously in prisons, such as the infamous Abu Ghraib. Indeed, CPT helped create the conditions that finally allowed the press to report on the horrendous abuses being carried out in Abu Ghraib and other prisons.

And when we last talked just three weeks before his death, Gene was mulling over the way in which Christians might make the most prophetic witness to the US Government concerning the war in Afghanistan. Where were the prophetic voices in that war, he was asking.

In recent years Gene spent much time writing blogs about issues of social justice and world peace. Many times after reading his blog, my feeling would be: let officials in Washington read and internalize these learnings. I kept being amazed at the fairness of his writing. Given all he had witnessed, he might have been forgiven some fiery rhetoric, if not a few cheap shots. But no, his writing was piercing in its anti-militaristic analysis and compassionate in his vision for healthier ways for our nation and our world to live.

And for all Gene had witnessed of war and conflict around the world, he somehow avoided cynicism. Deep down, Gene was a believer. He believed that, however slowly, however much in fits and starts, the arc of history bent toward justice, as Martin Luther King averred.

Indeed, Gene brimmed with warmth and laughter. He would make "schputt" (German expression for the act of self-deprecation) of himself and would warmly tease his friends. His large girth encompassed his body and his spirit. Gene loved people.

At the International Voluntary Services (IVS) work camp near Vung Tau, Vietnam:
John Sommer, Peter Hunting, Gene and Willi Meyers (1965)

READING THE SIGNS OF THE TIMES

E-mail correspondence with CPT in late 2005

Shining the light, breaking the silence, always puts perpetrators, state or otherwise, on notice that someone is watching. That has been a basic plank in all human rights and detainee release work.

In Iraq two obvious things stood out to me. The total absence of controls at the border in the first year of occupation was jolting. Was that an invitation to romantic fighters from around the world? In other words was there a conscious US decision to fight the war on terror in one locality, Iraq? Or did they just not get around to dealing with borders? The second observation involved the bombings of the UN, International Committee of the Red Cross (ICRC), Care, and the Jordanian Embassy. Each of these organizations had a critique of the war. After they were bombed they largely fled, along with the NGOs, many of whom also had a critique. CPT was one of the few NGOs left. The decision to stay meant that CPT was very exposed in a situation that was dangerous.

In a moment of crisis our natural instinct is to close down. But kidnappings and threats against people are the invitation to action. Furthermore, if one plays the percentages shining the light wins much more often than silence. But I don't promise that it always wins. Shadowy parts of government don't like to have people watch them, let alone disclose their nature and work. It makes them feel found out and angry. They know that their own employers often abandon them when that happens.

How do I know this? From 1963-67, I watched firsthand the shadowy way in which the US operated either directly or through advisors.

I first touched the underside about six months after arriving in Vietnam as a conscientious objector with International Voluntary Services. (IVS). I found myself in a Special Forces camp almost by accident as I was going about other duties. Special Forces were new then but they welcomed me and showered me with hospitality. While I was there two of their number came back from patrol. I asked, testing them, where they had been, and didn't get much answer except that they made several kills. So I said to myself, if I speak some Vietnamese and they don't, how come I can't tell who the Vietcong (VC) are—how do they know so much? I came to see a culture in the advisory body that bragged about cutting off ears, kills, etc. I had no idea what to do with this information. The advisors and the US Forces were publicly commissioned as noncombat people, strictly advisors. I still watched. There were more killings of Vietnamese, always blamed on VC but nothing was making sense. In one breath the VC were described as so brave and smart and in another breath they were terrorists. I still watched. In that period I began to hear about "teams" sponsored by the Special Forces and other official US groups.

One morning in the fall of 1965 I stopped by the regional USAID office in Nha Trang to find my mailbox stacked with an unusually large number of cables, all from the Saigon office. I picked up the first cable. It read, "Come to Saigon immediately." Peter Hunting was killed in an ambush outside of Can Tho.' I was shocked and became completely disoriented. I could not restrain the tears. Before my eyes I saw the faces of Vietnamese families whom I had witnessed receiving a message of the death of a son, a father, or a mother. I called to get a reservation on a military flight to Saigon, ran home to get clothes and whatever else might be needed. I got a flight on a C-123 loaded with soldiers and military gear. No sooner had I reached the airplane when I burst into tears and cried the whole way to Saigon, a considerable distance, perhaps a flight of more than one and a half hours. I hadn't cried like this in living memory. My whole body shook uncontrollably as the noisy craft bumped its way to Tan San Nhut Airport. To this moment I can feel an angel or the spirit of Peter with me.

At the time of my brother Pete Hunting's death in Vietnam, Gene was his closest friend. They had bought motorcycles together and planned adventures they would have after completing their terms with International Voluntary Services (IVS). Years later, Gene and I met and he played a part in the healing journey that became my memoir *Finding Pete*. Gene figures prominently in the story, which includes what he told me about resigning his position with IVS, facing the US press corps in Saigon, and leaving Vietnam to work for peace.

- *Jill Hunting, Sonoma, California*

By 1966 several people in IVS had been killed in ambushes and by other means. I didn't have adequate direct knowledge to question these events. I was watching. Then one of my colleagues, David, was assassinated in the delta. He was a particularly competent agriculturalist who worked in "insecure" areas and was known as the "poor American." We knew him to have connections on both sides. He was killed in very strange circumstances by soldiers dressed in VC black. No one wanted to investigate because the area was so insecure. But we received messages suggesting that it might not have been the VC. I watched and listened but didn't yet have a handle for response.

One day in early 1967 I was visiting an IVSer in Central Vietnam when a person who identified himself as from the Embassy came by to visit. We chatted amiably and he described his highly confidential work that included teams of soldier VC look alikes under his supervision and training. That was a moment of transformation for me. I spent a sleepless night trying to place a frame on the context of what I was seeing in front of my eyes but in the shadows of the war officially being fought by a half million American soldiers in uniform.

Other experiences like this led to my resignation in 1967. By then I realized that this was not a war between uniformed armies of regular units but was instead, a massive underground operation that included assassination and terror on both sides. I still didn't know what to do except to speak out. Our act of resignation gave us enormously improved access to Vietnamese. People shared their experiences and details about relatives who were either killed or disappeared. Events like My Lai were occurring with regularity so some of the Vietnamese and IVSers and others on the fringe started to work with the press to get these stories out. In that period, some foreign workers like me were able to make contact, very carefully, with the underground.

Also it was during that period that Doug Hostetter, a worker with Mennonite Central Committee, was threatened by—if I am not mistaken—Americans working in his area. Other IVSers were suspected for their lack of loyalty. The departure of some of us was encouraged so that we could speak out while others remained.

Gradually, way too gradually, I accepted the fact that my friend David had been killed by one of those U.S. secret teams in the delta. I had not said anything at the time but the truth settled in and was reinforced as other Vietnamese and a few internationals disappeared.

We worked hard to tell our story and we found Congress interested because we had been there. We learned to work with specific incidents and situations like the Tiger Cages, an Abu Ghraib type facility. Occasionally we had a little success through a combination of contacting friendly people in Congress, in the State Department, and by pushing the press.

One day while working in Washington, I went to the State Department to discuss a specific case with a friendly desk man. In our conversation and commiserations over the war, he handed me a paper that had just come to his desk. It was a report on human rights in Vietnam. He thought he was doing me a favor. What he didn't know was that the original of that paper had come to my desk two days earlier from a friend in Vietnam and that he was now giving me a copy of a paper that only I had. In fact, the paper had my scribbling on the top. I didn't say anything but I realized that the copy center downstairs probably had more than one employer and from then on I was more discreet.

Our work on the war always had two phases; one was pressuring Congress and the second was speaking out in public. Both, we felt, were necessary. In those days we didn't assume that Congress was our enemy or that everyone in the State Department was CIA or that people in government

> I always felt a special bond based on having shared very formative years in the 1960s as one of the small group of IVSers who went to Vietnam together in 1963. I remember in 1967, when I returned to Vietnam just before Gene, Willi Meyers, John Sommer and Chief of Party Don Luce decided they needed to resign from IVS in a public way, that Gene asked me if I felt abandoned by these four old friends. It was characteristic of his sensitivity to the range of effects of one's actions at a time when most of us would push forward without concern for ramifications of our behavior beyond our main intentions.
>
> – *Carlie Numi,*
> *Kennet Square, Pennsylvania*

were bad unless proven good. In fact we rather liked a lot of those folks and probably naively thought that when the war was over we would all go back to working together as before.

In the late 1970s my work in the Philippines led me through similar close contact with vicious detention, interrogation, and assassination. I can't tell you how many conversations Dorothy and I had with people affected. The prevailing notion then was to go as public as possible as fast as possible with information of these abuses. Filipinos were really good at that. Later, at Synapses we went public much more systematically and had a little success in helping surface Filipino political detainees—Karl Gaspar, Myrla Baldonado and others—when they were being held incommunicado. Sometimes we would just pick up the phone and call the military commanders in the Philippines directly. Sometimes we would send faxes to the homes of the commanders all with the notion that they needed to know that the world was watching.

While each situation in countries where I've worked from Vietnam to Philippines to Iraq has its political and cultural particularities and unique nuances, one actor has remained the same: United States. I am struck by threads of similarity. It took me years in Vietnam to make some sense of what I was seeing. So I understand why many people do not readily read the signs of the times from this perspective.

REMEMBERING THE LITTLE BOY

August 4, 2009

On August 15, 1945 I was five-and-a-half years old. My mother and I were in the house when the news arrived by radio. I didn't realize that it was so important. I had never known a time in my life when there was no war. War was normal and it didn't affect me except for the brown sugar we had to use for our cereal instead of white. My mother asked me to run to the barn and tell Dad that the war was over. I felt urgency in her voice.

I ran out the cement sidewalk to the barn and tried to find my father. Going to the barn with a message was normal. Usually it was about someone in the community or church. Occasionally it was about an emergency that my father, a minister, needed to tend to. This time was different because it had to do with the whole world. So I ran as fast as I could. He wasn't in the barn so I looked in the milk house and then the granary, the shop, and the chicken house. Finally I found him on the barn bridge repairing something.

Out of breath I ran up the bridge as fast I could. "Mom said I should tell you the war is over." There it was, I had said it. Dad looked down at me and said, "Oh, I am so glad." He said it again, "I am so glad." His response seemed strange because usually when I delivered a message, he would race off to the car, or to the house to make a telephone call, and I would race after him to get in on the action. "Oh, I am so glad," he said again, and then was silent. In the distance we heard the sound of explosions and Dad said, "I think they are celebrating the end of the war." I was confused because I didn't understand the meaning of the word "celebrate." But my mission was completed.

My final words to Dad that day were, "But who won?" His answer, "Nobody won." For months, I wandered around trying to understand why "nobody won."

The Little Boy in me is still contemplating how nobody could win. Little Boy was the name of the bomb that exploded over Hiroshima on August 6, 1945, nine days before my mother sent me on my first war-ending mission. Some people may have forgotten the name of the bomb that hit Japan. Most of us may never have known its name.

The images of incinerated Japanese children, parents, soldiers, buildings, and playgrounds never get easier to look at. The bomb that destroyed so much within us and killed so many was built by the Manhattan Project incorporating the work of 130,000 people. The 5-ton bomb exploded 1,900 feet above Hiroshima, directly over a parade field where Japanese soldiers were doing calisthenics at approximately 8:15 a.m. The B-29, piloted by Colonel Paul Tibbet and named Enola Gay in honor of his mother's favorite fictional character, was already 111/2 miles away when it felt the shock of the blast. At first, Tibbet thought his airplane was taking flak. After the second shock wave the crew looked back at the city and described what they saw. "The city was hidden by that awful cloud... boiling up, mushrooming, terrible, and incredibly tall."

The spiritual cloud of Little Boy from the misted-over memory of my childhood now hovers over all of us. Colonel Tibbet retired in Columbus,

Ohio, the city where I joined American Mennonites last month for the biennial church assembly. About piloting the Enola Gay he said, "I'm proud that I was able to start with nothing, plan it, and have it work as perfectly as it did... I sleep clearly every night." Shortly before his death in 2005 he said, "If you give me the same circumstances, I'd do it again."

I still want to deliver my own Little Boy message of August 15, 1945, because the war set in motion by the Hiroshima event is not over. Almost all of us recognize how dangerous it has become. Most of us know that the chance of more Hiroshima explosions anywhere in the world remains very high. So we push it from our memory or leave it to government authorities, who work in secret. Sixty-four years ago it took an effort the size of the car industry of the time to build and deliver the nuclear bomb. Today it would take only a handful of motivated and reasonably educated people to deliver one. Moral conviction, combined with the fear that we may not survive, has so far held us back. But that dam may break.

"Nobody won," a teaching passed on to me by my father and passed to him from generations before, hints at another way of thinking about winners and losers, attack, revenge, and enemy work. On that day 64 years ago, Dad started to teach me to suspend my instantaneous need for judgment, punishment, and pride of victory. Sometimes I remember to practice these lessons. That is also when hope settles over me and I can see a unity in the cosmos that may reach beyond my generation.

BEYOND IMAGINATION

May 4, 2006

The value that we put on life in a war situation—now the Iraq war—stretches us to the roots of the meaning of our lives. I grew up in a home where great respect was shown for Anabaptists who died for their faith. (Anabaptists are the free church ancestors of many evangelicals, including Baptists, Brethren, and Mennonites.) An estimated 5000 of them died during their formative era in the 16th century and since. As a child, I would sometimes go into my father's study and take down the biggest book there, an old copy of the *Martyrs Mirror,* which had been given to him by his father. I would look at some of the drawings depicting horrible scenes of torture and killing. Then I would read one or two of the stories of how my spiritual ancestors, Anabaptists and others, lived and died because of their faith. I was very impressed with their courage, boldness, and authenticity.

Occasionally I would ask about the stories and would get respectful, serious confirmation that, yes, these people who lived courageously and died by the thousands were in fact my ancestors. Then I would go about my life on the farm, engage in baseball fantasies and play football. Sometimes I took a long walk in the woods to try to understand what it would be like to live in a world where my convictions could get me killed. I was troubled by the thought that I might not have the courage to follow through. And also by the thought that I might have that kind of courage. Which was worse?

One of the dangerous things that Anabaptists did was to read the Bible and notice what it said. This was one source of their courage. The gospel, because of its inherent content, is described as an offense, meaning that it is a challenge to authority that threatens governments and institutions. The Anabaptists read about losing life in order to save it. Like their distant enlightened modern cousins they may have initially wondered what was meant by the phrase, "Unless a kernel of wheat falls to the ground and dies, it remains only a single seed. But if it dies it produces many seeds (John 12:24)." I don't think that they understood this as referring to a new kind of commercial or organic fertilizer. Their lives demonstrated this teaching as referring to the end of life for a specific living seed, a symbol for Jesus and his followers.

Anabaptist conviction and witness carried the threat of death because the Anabaptist understanding of faith did not smoothly interface with the political and social systems of the Holy Roman Empire. Anabaptist commitment to voluntarism and nonviolence was an offense to the system. Religion and empire worship were intertwined and there was little tolerance for deviation from the norm. Something in their world view gave these folks courage and calm. Although they argued for rights and for freedom of belief, they could not have known that their work was part of the bedrock that in future centuries would lead to a fundamental change in the way people understood rights of all kinds. Their willingness to accept death was a product of a comprehensive view that the meaning of an individual life reaches beyond the boundaries of this earthly body.

Anabaptist conviction was expressed in a time that predated the Enlightenment, which taught us that the only reality is material reality, that life ends with death, and that everything is explainable if you just have enough scientific knowledge. Such a perspective is very different from one that says some part of us goes on beyond this earthly life. Today this extension of physical life is discussed in the language of energy and quantum physics, avenues that may not be completely disconnected from the stuff of salvation which we read about in the Bible.

Our modern notions of Human Rights and economic rights have been formed in a milieu of modern materialism. Economic rights say that it is your good fortune to live in a time when the accumulation of wealth is good. You get there by being smarter, working harder or just being born in a place where the momentum is on the side of wealth, your personal wealth. A liberal Human Rights perspective says that the material manifestation of life must be preserved at all cost. It states that life is valuable, deserving of respect and honor. The taking of life by the state or by individuals or groups is bad but sometimes necessary. The pacifist works on this continuum but pushes it out a bit further by saying that it is never right to take life. Today most pacifists function unconsciously within the world view of the Enlightenment

It is good to occasionally check in with the people in our ancestry who thought there were things worth living and dying for. Their lives—albeit in historical periods with very different world views—help us see the deeper meaning of the life, faith, and worldwide perspectives waiting to be revealed within us. Their lives also help us to get back to the often analyzed but rarely lived Gospel which describes the power of light, which I take to be the light of God. Light is always more powerful than darkness. Telling truth when everyone around you is lying is dangerous but very powerful. Once that truth is out, it is almost impossible to stop it. Something has to be done. Either you get rid of the truth teller or you start rumors. In modern times you can use the media for this. The truth teller is naive, misled, or ungrateful to the military that is the source of power.

It should not surprise us that peacemakers who are killed in dangerous situations evoke hostile responses. Most societies do not yet function out of a world view that the light that flows through our material bodies and beyond will prevail. Such a perspective is an irritant. But we know the perspective of light points to a hopeful way out of violence by reminding us that we may not be chained forever to the limits of our material imaginations.

LETTER TO PARENTS

(EXCERPT)

January 27, 1969

Gene's time in Washington, DC (1967-72) was not only politically intense as he worked with others to stop the Vietnam War, it was also a time of dealing with post traumatic stress from his years in a war zone, and a time of his forging a new kind of relationship with his family and with the religious foundations of his childhood.

Dear Mom and Dad,

Although these past few months have been most painful they have provided long overdue insights into the nature of life. Surrounded so often by fear and repressed emotion, we are driven beyond ourselves to the unknown.

For years much that might have happened in our relationship has not happened, for reasons beyond the grasp of us all. We took each other for the roles we expected each other to play and not for being the human beings we are. As the youngest in the family I came at a busy and frantic time when a new house was built and the church had to be tended. Sometimes love was lost in the more immediate pressures.

Your letter Mom was very touching and I accept your pleas for forgiveness. When I moved into my present house, a girlfriend gave me a plant for my room. The plant has become very important for me because in caring for the plant I have come to accept you and the growth that is possible in a relationship that destiny has given me.

Not only have I come to appreciate you, but I have come to appreciate womanhood and motherhood and all that is so beautifully feminine about this world. And this discovery is one of the most rewarding and exciting that any male fumbling on the brink of manhood can ever make.

I only hope I can also forgive myself and that you can forgive me for being so crude and destructive. But now it is history and that is the way it had to be written. I can never "cast everything in the sea of forgetfulness." But I can accept and move on and learn from it all.

As I said when I was home, the basic principles of life were given to me by both of you, mom and dad, and these principles continue to guide my life. It may perplex you at times that the blueprint is not what you expect it to be, but you will remember that I am a product of another generation and that my home can never be limited to the Mennonite fold. It might be warm and secure to settle down in a pastoral Mennonite community, but that would never satisfy my energy and the demands of my soul. The world is my home.

The months ahead will be exciting and difficult because I will need to make some decisions and move on to the next step. There is no rush to do this, and I will allow the decisions to rise out of the heart when and where they will.

Love, Gene

The Stoltzfus Family

RETURNING TO ROOTS

From various emails
and article fragments, 2005

I returned to the Mennonite Biblical Seminary in Elkhart, Indiana in the fall of 1972. This return to my roots was timely. I had figured out how war works and how the big political games are played. Now I began to deepen my understanding of how the road of faith can be built to intersect with the world socially and politically, so that the possibilities of nonviolent engagement will show real gains.

By that time I had also come to a completely new understanding of why Jesus died. My answer flowed directly from my thinking about nonviolence and its inherent connection to a lifetime commitment of faith. My reasoning went something like this: Jesus' ministry was on the edge of village life where it brazenly and lovingly confronted hypocrisy, sickness, and injustice. His style incorporated symbolic actions, words of confrontation, and poetic or parabolic teachings which awakened the deeper recesses of the minds and souls of his audience. He also did little healing exercises sometimes, called miracles.

Jesus' teachings, and more profoundly his actions were built on several centuries of prophetic imagination in Jewish life, and were potentially very dangerous to the religious, economic, and political order of the time. That idea was not particularly hard to comprehend since I had been functioning within a manipulative and terror-guided world for the last ten years in Vietnam and in Washington, DC during the war. It was not a great leap for me to understand that people get killed for challenging the system of terror and economic control. What was different about Jesus was the methodology of his march through the villages and on to Jerusalem. I realized that his life could not be fully comprehended without some deeper spiritual wisdom.

PART II

CIRCLING THE GLOBE

Though we have conveniently titled the following sub-sections "Home-front" and "Around the World," for Gene each experience was local, whether in Chicago, Manila, Chiapas, Hebron, Peshawar or Fort Frances. His blog entries, letters, public statements, speeches, and articles presented here help to clarify Gene's sense of the inter-connectedness of war, poverty, and racism. But this is not a hand wringing about world problems. Gene's guiding perspective is that of an engaged peacemaker responding with clear eyes and an open heart to the pains and dreams and struggles of people in their own setting.

Section A

HOMEFRONT

SEEING THE CITY

Reprinted from *The Other Side* Magazine,
January-February, 1985

It was last January, just as a new batch of students was arriving, that I detected a timid knock on the door of my office at Chicago's Urban Life Center. Outside I found a student and her mother. They wanted to see the house, deep on the south side of Chicago, that serves as the center's living quarters and classroom space. So one of the staff, between the clutter of suitcases, bunk beds and ringing telephones, gave them a quick introduction. After the tour, we offered to carry in the young woman's baggage. She declined, saying that she and her mother wanted to go to a restaurant to get something to eat first. They'd return later.

In about an hour my phone rang. It was the student. She spoke only twelve words. "This is Jeannie," she said. "I won't be coming to the center this term." Before I could ask her why, she hung up the phone. Had she been frightened by the inevitable confusion of opening day? Had she been put off by the blackness of our neighbors' skin? Had she judged our program to be an inadequate bridge to the urban culture? I realized I would never know.

One thing I do know is that for me, the city has become an encouraging network of friends and co-workers. Oh yes, I see incredible injustice. But I also see wide margins of opportunity for growth. Not too many years ago I, too, was a stranger to Chicago. But it has come to be home. Despite the city's diversity and sometimes impersonality, I have found a village to which I can belong. I have found black brothers and sisters who share with me their histories and dreams. I have found Spanish-speaking colleagues who remind me of the debt this nation owes to the people of Mexico and Puerto Rico, and other parts of Latin America. And I have found Asian friends.

Yet each case of the vanishing student—and there have been several—is important. Such incidents call me back to my task. They're a reminder that, although for me the city is home, for others it's an empty hole filled in their minds with irrational crime, undisciplined ethnic groups, corrupt government, and hate-filled armies of youths who foist their violent urges on whoever may be available.

Some time ago, I asked several students what kind of nocturnal dreams they had about coming to the city. Their collective answer offered pictures of hate-filled monsters stalking the streets, horrible encounters with nameless vampires, and dangerous temptations into the depths of sin. For some, the images were sufficiently evil that only a superhuman act of choice had allowed them to fulfill the commitment they had made to themselves to spend one term of their college career with us.

Does that perverse, awful monster of the city, lurking in the irrational depths of so many people, explain the mad dash from our house by this most desperate student? Will she now join that great mass of Americans who come to Chicago—speeding past its neighborhoods, its immigrants, its collage of strange tongues—to patronize the exclusive shops of Water Tower Place? And after cheering our beloved Cubs to another rousing defeat, will she rush out after a sandwich at McDonald's, never even dreaming of tasting our abundant ethnic food? Will she settle down to a good life elsewhere—and teach her children those same fears that she has been taught?

Unfortunately, it's not just ethnic food one misses when one runs from the mythological urban monster. It's also a perspective on reality. Chicago is no longer Hog Butcher of the World or a Stacker of Wheat. The Big Shoulders that Carl Sandburg saw are gone now. What is left are deteriorating buildings, long-abandoned factory hulks, and an endless succession of neighborhoods made up of the lucky and the unlucky—those who have jobs and those who don't. Chicago, like any big city, is people. It's people looking for a place to use their energy. It's people looking for jobs. It's people—in a nation that bulldozes half a million living units a year—simply looking for a place to live.

Some years ago, as a Christian worker in Southeast Asia, I asked some friends what I could say to my brothers and sisters in North America about the oppression of the poor in Southeast Asia. They said I should try again to help people in my own country understand why it is that millions of American Blacks are poorer than their white counterparts.

Nothing provides a clearer look at the world's economic system than a large American city. The corporations that once provided jobs in Chicago are now in Southeast Asia searching for low-priced labor and high-yielding tax breaks. The meat packers, the steel producers, the lumber merchandisers—they are leaving the cities of North America for the emerging industrial zones on the economic periphery of our world.

> I learned that I don't even get to see that which is new if I try too hard and too quickly to force everything into logical, pre-existent categories in this brain I carry around.
>
> - *January 10, 2007*

Of course they are careful not to sink their foundations too deep any-where. They are always ready to pick up and move again to more favorable territory where government can assure cheaper labor, fewer restrictions, and lower taxes. Corporations are driven by a desire to maximize profits and control resources. So if wages in Chicago seem high compared to those in Mexico, these companies simply pull out. Local politicians, whether they be third-world dictators or machine-controlled mayors, are pitted against one another in gaining jobs for their citizens.

When I was in the Philippines, I visited an export processing zone where Barbie dolls and fenders for Ford cars were made. In that zone, American and Japanese corporations enjoy the benefits of cheap labor—labor that is prevented from organizing by strong-arm rule. If a revolutionary government should come to power, the companies would quickly move on to countries where less pro-people policies are in effect. Today, with President Reagan promoting "urban enterprise zones" for our job-short cities, we've come full circle. The policies that have worked successfully for corporations overseas are being brought home. American's poor are being made to roll over and beg for corporate tax breaks, a sub minimum wage, and weakened labor organizations.

If the Urban Life Center were to post a sign saying we had ten jobs available at four dollars per hour, we'd be inundated with five hundred applications or more. Folks are desperate. Imagine supporting a family of five on four dollars an hour! During the winter months, fuel costs alone would eat up a third of your income. In Chicago—in any big city—we're confronted with a sad truth. This land of wealth and opportunity can no longer deliver on its promise. There aren't enough jobs even for the college educated!

It wasn't an aesthetic preference for light skin over dark that embedded racism so deeply into our civilization. And it wasn't the misuse of one or two verses in the Bible that caused it either. No, the slavery of Black people came into being because our economic system required cheap labor. If there hadn't been Blacks available, we would have found someone else. Color was just the handy way we segmented the cheap-labor people from the high-living people.

To this day, the legacy of slavery poisons black-white relations. And just as we struggle to heal the wounds of centuries, future generations will be forced to heal the wounds we're now inflicting on the underclass of our own society. In the name of profits, we're continuing to marginalize a whole segment of our society, the urban poor, and the vulnerable hungry who, in a desperate bid to survive, will do whatever their corporate masters say.

Can we white middle-class Christians do anything? No, not if we run from the city, not if we deny reality, not if we ignore the sins of the past. To stem the tide, to reverse the flow, we must recognize the depth of slavery—the depth of slavery that still runs through our system. Then we must have faith. We must have faith in what God can do through us. We must catch the biblical vision of a city in which justice is the norm, a city in which no stone is left unturned in an effort to provide a fair living for all.

How do we help? We help when, like Jesus, we become friends of the victims. We help when, in the midst of that friendship, we release our skills and work as allies not managers. We help when, by unleashing our energy, we create joy in simplicity. We help when, in the midst of impending violence, we celebrate the God of justice.

It's a perverted culture that views education as a means to self-advancement. Through education we acquire tools to serve others. That service helps most when it's offered at the bottom. We make the biggest difference when we have broken free from all forms of exploitation, when we ourselves have turned from every slavery-promoting tendency that dominates and threatens to destroy our society. The less we have to protect in terms of life-style, personal security, reputation, or family, the easier it will be.

A journey into the city takes us into opportunities for action and creativity that we never expected. We are confronted with our white privilege attitudes in ways that we never anticipated. We despair that anything good can come from our efforts. Some firmly held attitudes are shattered. Our faith is tested. But if we believe—as I do—that the meek shall inherit the earth, then we can survive. Then we can flourish. The journey of faith, the journey of hope, can begin with the simple assertion that the world was made for us all. The only way it can be kept in safety is for all of us to share in the control of, and access to, its wealth and resources.

As I work on problems in Chicago, I often remember that in the Philippines, strategic hamlets are being created, modeled after the pacification projects of Vietnam. Those hamlets failed to pacify the hopes of the people of Vietnam. And they will fail in the Philippines. Yet the effort goes on. Farmers are hounded into village centers, far from their fields, where they're watched from dusk to dawn to keep them from supporting insurgents.

Why do I think of the Philippines while encountering the poverty and despair of Chicago? Because money freed up by the closing of shops and factories here has provided the capital for export farming there—export farming on the very land from which those Filipino farmers have been driven. As a result, we get to eat a bit more cheaply. And, not so incidentally, the pockets of the businesses involved get to grow a whole lot fatter. We're all victims of this nonsense—students who can't find work, the long-term unemployed, welfare recipients, and peasant farmers killed or driven from their land in the third world. To see the problems of Chicago is to see the problems of a worldwide economic system gone awry.

To some, seeing the problem is the beginning of despair. For me, to see the problem is the beginning of hope. For I believe the dollars that created the urban monster of our dreams can be redirected. I believe God is calling us to catch a new vision of a city where black and white, Asian and European, will celebrate life together. It's a city in which the children of welfare mothers play and are schooled together with the children of the rich.

I only have hunches about how that will happen. Capitalism says that the bourgeois are most capable of bringing in that new day. Marx has suggested that working people will be the harbingers of a new age. And Christ said that the meek will inherit the earth. May our faith give us the energy and perseverance to be a part of the solution. May the monster in our dreams be transformed. By a Lamb.

Vietnam (2009)

COOK COUNTY COURT STATEMENT

June 7, 1988. Chicago, Cook County Circuit Court. The 1980s was an era of US military interventions in Central America funded by US tax dollars. The peace and justice community across the country used many avenues to draw attention to the bloodshed and the atrocities with an eye to ending the US interventions and covert wars. Gene, along with twelve others, was charged with criminal trespass for singing Central America-themed carols during the Christmas rush at Water Tower Place, a high end shopping center on Michigan Avenue's Magnificent Mile. Later, when the case was taken to the Illinois Supreme Court and charges dismissed, the three judges requested the peace defendants to sing carols for them.

"Your honor, I am 47 years old and have spent half of my adult life traveling in more than 30 countries around the world. I have clear and strong feelings about the people with whom I have worked. They are struggling for an economic chance. I have been in hundreds of marketplaces around the world. They reach back more than 4,000 years and are institutions for exchanging goods, services, and ideas. Your honor, only in this country have I been arrested for exchanging ideas in the marketplace. When I walked into Water Tower Place to sing, I carried with me my colleagues from around the world. And in this season of peace I choose to remember them.

Your honor, my first American ancestor came here in 1764. I can look back through seven generations of Mennonite ministers who have lived in this land. My foreparents came here in order to gain religious freedom and economic opportunity, and to escape persecution—the same reasons for which people are struggling in places like Central America. Many were tortured and some died because of their convictions. I am proud to spring from these roots. America has been very good to me. But when I measure its kindness to me against its treatment of my friends in other lands, my pride turns to ambivalence.

Your honor, the marketplace has historically been the site where punishment is carried out. If you choose to punish me, I would invite you to consider having me manacled and placed in the mezzanine of Water Tower Place for a period of not less than one month."

Gene and Debbie Johnson at Shine the Light Vigil, Washington, DC January 2006

The adapted versions of "Away in a Manger," focusing on US military intervention and "Holy, Holy, Holy" focusing on the US economic embargo of Nicaragua, are two of the many carols and hymns Gene and others sang in public places.

Away in a Manger

Away in Honduras the bases are built
Increasing war's danger, increasing our guilt
We will not continue to bankroll this war
The people must surely say "Basta! No More!"

Away in Guatemala the military's thrust
Is slaughter of Indians, they learned it from us
We will not continue to bankroll this war
The people are crying out "Basta! No More!"

Holy, Holy, Holy

Coffee, coffee, coffee
Nicaraguan coffee
Brought by boat from overseas
We buy it by the case
Served fresh or reheated
Injustice thus defeated
   Brewed strong by perk or drip!
      Elec-tric-ally

LETTER TO THE INTERNAL REVENUE SERVICE

Gene was a war tax resister beginning with the Vietnam War and he tried to keep open those possibilities for others in whatever organization he worked. Every April, if his income was large enough to be taxed, he wrote the Internal Revenue Service (IRS) to explain that he was a conscientious war tax resister. Sometimes he invited the IRS to join him in refusing to fund wars.

April 2, 2008
Internal Revenue Service
USA

To whom this may concern:

Attached you will find my tax return. You will notice that the enclosed check represents 50% of what your systems lead me to believe that I owe. I will not be paying the balance now, or ever, because I do not regard the 50% allocated to national security, as well as to past, present, and future wars to be a responsible investment into security for any of us. I have been a conscientious objector to war and have practiced nonviolence. I would be most grateful if you would simply forgive this portion of my tax. If you choose not to do so, I will have no other choice but to seek a presidential pardon! Thank you for your attention to this matter and to the matters of the nation...

Respectfully,
Mervin E. Stoltzfus

On peace speaking tour, Waterloo train station, UK, (2009)

PEACEMAKER WHEELS

April 17, 2009

Last week, I visited three communities in the Great Plains as part of a Wheels of Justice bus tour, traveling in a made-over 56-passenger bus. At stops in Denver, Wichita, and Manhattan, Kansas our 100-gallon tank was filled with fuel made from soy. The clown-like bus had animal life painted on its sides, and words of hope such as, "War is not the Answer!" Our bus made us a hit, an instant enemy, and mostly a curiosity in every town.

We traveled in this way to elicit conversations on war and peace. The mission of Wheels of Justice, now approaching eight years of crisscrossing the country, is to tease the nation away from war. The bus is driven by Bill Hill, 62, a foster child, Vietnam War veteran, and single father who raised two daughters. Bill learned to manage big machines as a tank driver with the 3rd Tank Battalion of the 3rd Marine Division in Da Nang, Vietnam. He helps two speakers on the bus's traveling team by telling his story, which includes combat, addictions, and war memories buried deep in his mind.

On this trip I mostly told stories of Iraqi families and their children who are still disappearing into the catacombs of US and Iraqi prisons. I spoke about Iraq and another team member spoke about Palestine, and together we wove the threads of war, terror, and smart bombs in the Middle East and in the US. We nudged our audiences to remember that comprehensive solutions lead back to dealing with the US government's unbalanced support for Zionism as expressed in Israel.

A brightly painted bus gets attention. After getting people to notice, you must keep their attention long enough to motivate them to do real long term work. Thirty-eight years ago I helped organize the Indochina Mobile Education Project, which did, in another war period, some of what Wheels of Justice tries to do today.

We equipped a VW minivan with 24 display panels showing everyday life for Vietnamese people and the effects of war. Over five years the exhibits appeared in 350 shopping centers across the country. Vietnam hands, civilian and military, Vietnamese and Americans who had been through the war spoke in schools, colleges, churches, service clubs, and community meetings. I wish we could have been a little more creative, but I think one reason we didn't spice up the paint on our VW was because we preferred not to have our vans trashed by people who hated our message. Several times the traveling team called me to prepare a replacement display panel that had been spray painted or destroyed by upset citizens.

Often I jumped into my aging Volvo and traveled to a future display site, put on my only suit and went with local people to meet the mall manager armed with letters of blessing and recommendations from important personalities and other, supportive mall managers. Often the negotiations were protracted. Occasionally when we suggested that the media might be interested in the success of our local display and special Vietnamese dinner, the door got nudged open a little bit further.

Gene was our anchor – a person who kept us grounded – through IVS days, the Indochina Mobile Education Project, the Indochina Resource Center, and beyond. What a privilege to have known him. He'll live on in all of us he touched.

- *John Spragens, Eugene, Oregon*

By combining the visuals of a display, the sounds of our voices, the touch of materials from Vietnam with the taste of Vietnamese food we learned how to light some flames. The steps to creating a recipe for conversations about the signs of the times are as difficult on the Wheels of Justice as they were with our fledgling efforts 40 years ago.

One thing these two projects have in common: we met veterans newly returned from war who were trying to put their lives together and escape the memories. I always looked for a better way to include their pain and harsh memories in the trek across our country. By telling his story, Bill Hill, the driver, helped me get closer to an answer.

"War is not the answer," and "Occupation: the Roadmap to Nowhere" cried out from the side of our bus. As we traveled I watched spring unfold and saw lush green wheat fields drinking up the sparse sunshine. These are the fields where settlers met and their government betrayed, native people. In those days

the earth sometimes shook. In the fields today I saw another future: the children of clashes becoming the prophets of hope.

Wheels of Justice bus.

HONORING CONSCIENCE IN AUSTIN, TEXAS

Oct 9, 2009

Two weeks ago I spoke at a gathering in Austin, Texas, on Honoring Conscience. In Austin we celebrated acts of conscience in an honoring ceremony where persons from many walks of life—former soldiers, tax resisters, community activists, educators, professionals, workers, and conscientious objectors—gathered for special words of blessing. An important spirit behind the celebration of conscience was Garland Robertson, former air force pilot and chaplain. As a Lieutenant Colonel he had reached an internal boundary that would not allow him to go on if he did not publicly acknowledge his emerging convictions about militarism.

As the words of recognition were spoken, my mind was also illuminated by a cloud of witnesses from every clan and culture with whom I had worked and from every nation where I had served. I remembered the Iraqi soldier I met in Baghdad who refused to serve in Iraq's army. His ear was partially cut off as a permanent reminder of his disobedience. I remembered the paramilitary soldier in Columbia who showed up one day seeking help to disappear from his comrades who would surely kill him if they knew he was trying to leave. I remembered the local pastors, prophets, imams, monks, and human rights workers who listened to conscience and saved lives in the Philippines, Vietnam, Burma, and Indonesia, each in a special time of political emergency. In Pakistan this past June I met a Pukhtoon man from the part of Pakistan where the Taliban are strong, who traveled for two days by foot and bus to tell the story of the bombing that his people live under and to plead for help in saving lives.

On November 11, 2010, the local Fort Frances Anglican priest, Fr Wayne MacIntosh laid a wreath for Gene as a Christian Peacemaker at the annual Remembrance Day Service at the Legion. Jackie Guimond, a local musician and member of Call to Action suggested this novel idea to the Legion and paid for the wreath. The local paper listed Gene's wreath immediately after those placed by the branches of the Armed Forces and before the Chamber of Commerce wreath.

It was humbling, in Austin, Texas, to be in the presence of this sacred trust of inner light, a force more powerful than law or might.

FROM NORTHWESTERN ONTARIO, HOMELAND OF THE ANISHINAABE PEOPLE

In 2004 Gene was delighted to move to Northwestern Ontario, homeland of Treaty Three Anishinaabe People. The time spent here, observing, attending events and discussions, and making friends convinced him the most creative thinking and action in this District was centered in First Nations communities. This interaction also led him to examine more closely what it meant for him as a descendant of European settlers to live on land stolen through violence and deceit, and to get a sense of the effects of the collective loss of culture, language and land on First Nations people. His writings reflected Gene's search for a path to make amends.

FIRST NATIONS PEOPLE: COMPENSATION AND APOLOGY

October 17, 2007

Some months after I moved to Ontario in 2004, the Canadian government announced a two-billion dollar legal settlement for native people who experienced abuse while attending government supported residential schools operated by churches over the last century. Depending upon the number of years in school and the abuse record, individuals will receive from $10,000 to $27,000 in claims that are now being processed across Canada. A little reported part of the settlement is the $60 million set aside for a Truth and Reconciliation Commission to provide opportunities in a safe environment for former students to speak about their Residential school experiences.

All of us have been instructed at an early age about forgiveness and many of us have had parents who led us through a process of apology. Forgiveness is the work that is done by the person or group who is offended. Apologies are offered by the person, group or nation who did the offending. In our childhood minds, these deeply rooted principles of right living are often confused and "mushed" together. Virtually every religion teaches forgiveness.

In an important final legacy of his life Jesus said, "Father, forgive them for they know not what they do."

Why do I connect the $2 billion dollar reparations payment to forgiveness and apology? The problem in the Americas is how the children of immigrants can build a healthy relationship with the First Nations peoples. We are living on land from which they were forcibly removed. In a time when we are all stretching for a new relationship to our earth, the world view of indigenous people is a timely gift, but are we ready to receive it? While the courts are heavily involved in land claims and matters such as this, residential schools reparations by themselves cannot make us get along. They can mandate rights or compensation, but that will not necessarily cleanse us from suspicions, put downs, and charges of unearned benefits. Orders backed by law can make us do things but force can never complete the work of apology or forgiveness.

One of the first stories I heard about my country came at school recess where I was introduced to the game, cowboys and Indians. I learned to be smart and strong and wanted to be a cowboy so that I could outwit the Indians. Is it too much for us to hope for a new day, a time when we celebrate for one another, even with one another?

I grew up in a home where apology and forgiveness were insisted on and at an early age I learned the power of three little words, "I am sorry." When I was about seven years old, a new boy began attending our church. For some reason I decided I didn't like the way this boy played and I decided to do something about it. After church one Sunday I goaded the boy into a totally unnecessary fight. I had learned how to fight and trick the opponent while playing cowboys and Indians. The fight went on outside the church in full view of church goers. I think I emerged victorious but like the victories at school, someone got hurt and, and it would take me years to work out the real consequences of the myth of cowboys and Indians.

The noon meal at our home was very quiet that Sunday. In another room I could hear hasty consultation between Mom and Dad. I knew that trouble lay ahead but I persisted in convincing myself that it was not about me. After the meal I was escorted from the kitchen by Dad. Now I knew there was trouble. Dad explained to me what a terrible thing I had done. My persistent denials were answered by very clear words from Dad and eventually the application of a paddle, a fairly rare mode of punishment in my growing up. There was more to come. Later that Sunday afternoon we drove to the home of the boy I had beat up where I was told to apologize to him in front of both sets of parents. I was mortified, but told myself I would get through this somehow. How come cowboys and Indians didn't work in real life, I wondered.

I said the magic words, including a specific sentence about the fight that I had been coached to say. There was long silence in the room. Then the boy's mother broke the silence by saying, "Oh isn't that cute." I remember the cute part because it struck me as stupid. I saw nothing cute about this entire episode. Her son was then coached to say the words of forgiveness and before long we were playing together again as though nothing had happened. Through the years I have never been sure when or if my apology became sincere. Like the governments who correct abuse with money I had learned to correct my abusive behaviour with the currency of ritualized words. To do so I needed a firm nudge from someone with more experience and power than I had. I now think that my parents did the right thing. It is hard however to dissolve the cowboy and Indian motif in the deep recesses of the mind.

The promise and process of Truth and Reconciliation (the name mandated by the government) leaves out the awkward actions required of most of us to get over our addiction to games like cowboys and Indians. The paddle of the law can give us a kick start. Actually Canada has a commendable record in dealing with non native minorities. But genuine peace has not yet been made with the First Nations.

In this, Canada is not unique. In all of the Americas there is the inclination to use money to treat these deep wounds of abuse and the legacy of unfair negotiations, forced assimilation, even genocide, before a cultural process of apology is fully engaged. Those of us who are descendants of immigrants have been living in denial and will need to walk through the pain of our own history to a new plane of truth and acknowledgment of unearned wealth and privilege. Although the settlement with victims of residential schools in Canada suggests reconciliation, it calls only for a process that creates a safe space for the school victims to tell their story. It says nothing about a process of transformation for the children of immigrants caught in our own addictions to subdue the earth for our economic benefit.

The spirit behind Truth and Reconciliation goes beyond charity to that place within us where we need to reconstruct our myth of how we got here, occupying this land. This is not a prescription for charity or therapy. It points us in a new direction. Lila Watson, an Australian Aboriginal leader has wise words for all of us. "If you have come to help me, you are wasting your time. But if you have come because your liberation is bound up in mine, then let us work together."

I participate in a Right Relations Circle, which has met monthly to reconnect with the hidden clumps of unfinished business in our own personal and cultural history. Last spring we visited a First Nations office where we were joined by local people. Our spokesperson presented a formal apology to First Nations People developed by the United Church of Canada. For the next six hours, amid tears and long silences First Nations people told personal stories of pain. One woman told of how her parents hid the children when the buses came to take them away to the schools. Another person spoke movingly of the experience of parents who had suffered from cultural prohibitions and brokenness in the residential schools. Several spoke of the loss of parenting skills only now being recovered because they had been removed from their homes at an early age. Others linked alcohol and drug abuse to the loss of family and to the sexual abuse experienced at residential schools.

The experience of speaking about hard memories in safe settings brings long suppressed pain to the light where its destructive power can be overcome with new personal power. This is the work of those who attended residential schools. Those who supported, paid for and benefited from residential schools also have hard work. Ours is the daunting task of getting in touch emotionally with what we actually apologize for. This is one step along the way to right relationships. Included will be our acknowledgement of the decimation of

I have participated...in many anti racism and diversity seminars. In these experiences I have noticed repeatedly how we white folks come prepared with our liberal notions and broad sweeping social statements while the emotional power of these sessions is supplied almost exclusively by people of color. White people need permission to delve into their own background, the hidden stories of unwholesome race relations in their own family lines, and the manner in which this secret history has been either passed on or covered up. I want to write a history of race relations in my own family.

- From Gene's e-mail, 2006

whole communities through war and smallpox spread by diseased blankets. Also included will be the story of the reduction of native populations from as many as 100 million people before Columbus was discovered in the Americas to a tiny percentage of that within a century.

Our Right Relations Circle has met to learn more of our own ragged history of gaining control of lands through devious promises, treaties, and resettlement schemes. We are learning to respond directly to the existing racist culture in every day life. "You know when 'they' get this money they will just use it to buy drugs or alcohol," said one neighbor to me over his fourth beer. As we work our way through this list of deadly statements and practice our responses, we believe we can be signs for a better relationship. Without this work we know that an apology is empty words. Other opportunities for engaging with First Nations may develop as we learn to demonstrate with our actions that we are safe and reliable allies.

Perhaps because soldiers only spend several weeks during basic training learning how to fight, some do not overcome their reluctance to kill, and find passive and active ways to avoid killing even during combat situations. Our culture has had five hundred years of basic training in the language, attitudes, and moral conscience of disregard for first people's integrity. It takes skill to undo old habits. I do not assume all the hard work has been done just because there is a legal settlement. I am still learning how to overcome the imprint of the games of my childhood.

GROWING UP ON CONQUERED LANDS

August 14, 2007

The August heat this year has reminded me of hot summer days in one of the fields on our farm in Aurora, Ohio where I grew up. The farm has long been overtaken by factories and suburban sprawl. But in my mind it is as fresh as it was 55 years ago when we took care of 25 cows and had just begun the transition to mechanized farming that included combines, tractors with rubber tires, and milking machines. Two parts of the farm remain firmly attached in my brain. The first is the maple sugar bush where we gathered sap every spring. I loved to skip school to help. The second is a field immediately to the north of the woods where we often found relics which we referred to as "Indian heads" (arrowheads, sometimes called flint heads) from a long forgotten native settlement. I never connected the two until recently.

We often found native artifacts in the field when we plowed in the spring or as we walked through the cornfield prior to harvest but had no idea how they got there, nor did we have any connection to the first dwellers. As far as we were concerned, we now owned the land. And these artifacts came from the distant past. In school we never learned about the native civilization that preceded us except as an addendum to the heroics of Euro-American personalities.

Our township was organized in 1807, 200 years ago and a full century before my own ancestors arrived to purchase the 137-acre farm. The discovery of native artifacts in the field beside the sugar bush always carried a kind of special power in our family. When we found an arrowhead it was considered a moment of triumph and word of the discovery quickly spread. Dad collected these special finds in a box.

I am not an archeologist but I suspect that the frequent discovery of native artifacts was evidence that a native village once occupied the field towards the back of our farm. The fate of that village has always bothered me. Who really owned "our" land? I found the existence of a previous people disconnected from my life unsettling. There was teaching in our church that the land belonged to God but I knew that somewhere in the mysterious offices of our county there was a legal deed of ownership that belonged to Stoltzfus. Through the years when I made my infrequent return visits to the farm land I would walk over that special field and try to listen to what the lingering spirits in the ground of that long forgotten village might be saying to me. But I never put the puzzle together.

I still want to know more about our farm's original dwellers. I google my native town, Aurora, but I find only references to a host of town committees, hotels, businesses, churches, and an item on town planning. Near the bottom of the list I find something called the Aurora Historical Society but it only has a reproduction of an early map, no reference to the first people. No help there. I continue to google my way through Native American history sites where I find hints about Erie, Shawnee, and other groups who lived in Northeast Ohio for a time after they were forced from their lands or defeated by conquering armies. So it is left to my imagination to make contact and peace with the first caretakers of our land who surely never sold it to anybody in the way we of European descent think of buying and selling. I make that leap in the best way I can by telling this story, particularly to native people when I meet them, as an offering, one of the things that just might make for peace in my generation.

Some years ago before I moved to Canada I learned that native people had been making maple syrup for as long as they could remember. Eventually I put this fact together with the maple trees beside our farm's native village and I suddenly realized that long before we harvested the spring sap from the maple trees, another people may have done so as well. Perhaps, long before my white ancestors settled in Ohio, and before they learned how to savor the sweet healthy harvest of maple syrup, the first people of Ohio settled in the field beside the sugar bush early every spring to conduct their harvest.

> This morning I will smoke my pipe and sing a song on my drum in honor of a wonderful man.
> - *Lori Flinders,* Weechi-it-te-win *Child and Family Services, Fort Frances, Ontario*

How do I make peace with the unearned benefits of conquered lands that have blessed me so much? My story is not complete, and I am in search of peace. I am still looking for the connection to that original village where maple syrup flows in abundance and where the conqueror and the conquered can find a pathway to fairness and plenty.

OUR WAY OF LIFE

Letter to the Editor of the
Fort Frances Times, August 26, 2009

It was the fourth council meeting in my township, Alberton, regarding a zoning change so that Weechi it te win, a native family services organization, could purchase a farm where it planned to open a new facility for youth. The room was full because the council was scheduled to vote. Scores of worried, angry people had spoken up and shouted out at the previous council meetings. "Our Way of Life" is threatened, said one young man who is starting a family. Across the highway from the projected facility, FOR SALE signs have appeared in several yards, a visible signal of protest, although the owners must not be serious because their prices are highly inflated.

I first learned the language of threat used with the phrase "Our Way of Life" during the 1950s. It emanated from white supremacists in Alabama as the civil rights movement heated up. My home was in Ohio. I knew segregation by race was wrong but couldn't figure out how it affected me and my way of life. So in the late 50s, as a student at Eastern Mennonite University (Virginia) I wrote and delivered a speech for an oratorical contest condemning segregation and racist thinking. It was actually a pretty safe thing to do. In those days we generally believed that racism was wrong but it didn't occur to us very often that people like me could do something about it. After the speech, a few people came to me to suggest that I might have stepped over the line and some people were offended. It was all very polite. Nothing like the doomsday, "our way of life" protests I felt in Alberton last week. Or maybe I just was not listening very well.

The other day I learned that some Americans are saying that Obama's health reform agenda is dangerous because it threatens our way of life. Although I am living in Canada where I enjoy public health care, I occasionally peek at American news where some commentators tell me how bad the Canadian health system is. I could not have learned this from my experience living here in Canada because for the first time in my life I go to the clinic for preventative checkups regularly. I have only lived here for five years so I might have a myopic view. In Chicago where I lived before, I only went to an emergency room if I was really sick, and I worried that they would clean out my billfold.

This ongoing tussle with the shadowy side of our common life brings me back home to this Alberton township (dispersed rural population 1000) where the council rejected the application for the native run youth facility on zoning grounds. The "Our Way of Life" people and the strict zoning interpreters on the council won out for now. I wonder what the council would have done if zoning changes were requested to pave the way

People gather for Walk Against Racism in Fort Frances, Ontario (2007)

for a university computer research facility. Would that fit into the Business Park zoning designation? That would have really challenged our way of life. And if the paper mill that employs 650 people would close or downsize, what would that do to zoning and our way of life.

Now in Alberton I am faced with the same "Our Way of Life" problem I faced fifty years ago when I was a student in Virginia. Do I stay quiet, keep the lawn mowed, and try to be nice to my neighbors? Do I make a sign "Natives, Non Natives, There is room for all of us," and walk or bicycle the forty or so miles of Alberton roads inviting my neighbors to a conversation? I am not sure how I feel about walking these roads alone. The tone of the meetings in the council chamber is stuck right now and the matter is not yet settled but what happened in Alabama tells me things don't stay stuck forever, even though Birmingham is not yet perfect.

> We here at the United Native Friendship Center (UNFC) will light a smudge and say a prayer for Gene.
> - *Sheila McMahon, Director UNFC, Fort Frances, Ontario*

The North American continent is stumbling towards a way of life that could be good for all of us. However, the unfinished project of equality and democracy sometimes gets in the way of our current way of life. The lawyers scramble for the spoils when we have disagreements like this. Law helps but it doesn't change my deeper side. I learned to try to be true to what is right in Sunday school a long time ago. I am not always successful. Education helps me sometimes but I forget very quickly. So how do I listen to my moral conviction and outrage, and help harvest them into a way of living that awakens the best in all of us—native, non native, timber worker, unemployed, professional, youth, and retired? Adjustments to an always changing "Way of Life" may be inconvenient in the short run but I know I can handle this walk only as I do it one step at a time, and as I invite my neighbors to walk with me.

ON THE ROADS OF ALBERTON TOWNSHIP

E-mail to Right Relations Circle, September, 2009

I was disappointed and shaken that the township council of Alberton had rejected the request for a zoning variance to accommodate the new Training Learning Center run by Weechi it te win Family Services, an agency that serves ten First Nation communities. I had to do something or else, I'd be depressed. I decided to make a sign for my bicycle and travel the roads of Alberton. I wanted my sign to awaken people's thinking but I knew that it could also evoke anger, hope, or boredom.

My bicycle has a motor on it. This creates curiosity in people who are tired of paying for gas. My beard also sets me apart. By adding a sign about native and non-native people getting along I was aware that my three pronged message symbol might be an overload and I worried that my message might be muted. To be honest, I also was a little concerned that I might encounter some angry people who would want to teach me a thing or two by word or deed.

My first sign, NATIVES—NON-NATIVES ROOM FOR ALL OF US IN ALBERTON, which Dorothy helped me design, turned out to be too big for the front of my bicycle. So back to the drawing boards we went. The second and smaller attempt felt more like a winner.

BIMOSETAA (Anishinaabemowin for "Let's walk")
NATIVE—NON-NATIVE
FORWARD TOGETHER

I have traveled the roads of Alberton, visited Fort Frances, Emo, International Falls, and Off Lake—probably about 300 kilometers total. No one has flashed me the V for victory sign, but no one has flashed the middle finger at me either. A few cars have waved approvingly but most looks are glum and non-committal. I can't tell if this indicates confusion, rejection, or suspended judgment.

Rainy River District in general and Alberton in particular is not a massive population center. I need to start thinking about a second edition to my sign to encourage the tiny interest that might have been planted. I need your suggestions. I don't want a sign that is so militant that no conversation is possible. I also don't want a sign with a message that induces sleep. I thought about turning my sign into a license plate from the local native population authorizing me to travel in this territory. Would that work? Help me think of the next edition!

If you meet me on the road remember to honk your horn and wave furiously so I don't develop "ambivalent rejection disorder" for which I would have to seek remedy in the Canadian health system, which in this instance may not be able to deliver healing.

As township residents, Gene and Dorothy also filed an appeal with the Ontario Municipal Board (OMB) which oversees local townships. Gene died before the final hearing, though his spirit was definitely present.

Though the appeal was dismissed on a technicality, the hearing officer also wrote, "... the Board urges the Township to consider carefully the objections and submissions of Ms. Friesen and the participants as their concerns are real." The OMB subsequently worked with the township to create a more inclusive land use planning document.

The story was covered by the Globe and Mail, a Toronto based national newspaper, and the academic journal, Ethnic and Racial Studies, will publish an essay on the Alberton group home controversy.

Section B

AROUND THE WORLD

THE EXCEPTIONAL AMERICAN

By Marilen Abesamis

It was 1976, the peak of Ferdinand Marcos' martial law, a time of social turmoil and deep political uncertainties in the Philippines. Not too many Americans dared to risk their lives with us, in the name of faith. But there was Gene Stoltzfus, smooth-shaven and cool in his batik cotton shirt, and sandals that could be dusted off quickly at the doorsteps. He had plunged into work in Davao City in the southern island of Mindanao with his young wife Dorothy Friesen, and both took on tasks as modern day missionaries of the Mennonite Central Committee, an entity we never heard of until then. "We" were the young professionals who had left the comforts of Manila to be with the poor in Mindanao, and Gene understandably dogged us with the question, "What drives you? What keeps you going?" It was as if he wanted to distill what was at the core of our mission, to hear the inner voice that animated us and made us see beyond the menacing faces of soldiers, grenades dangling at the waist, and the barbed checkpoints on every road.

Gene was an unobtrusive but comforting presence. He chuckled a lot at things that were new to him, but he never lectured nor admonished, never imposed. His gladsome presence was that of an enabler who read one's thoughts, and reflected them back in a clearer, more nuanced way. He had the gift of empowering people and seemed to accept women and men as they were, as jewels perfect in themselves, with no need for alteration. In his travels and research work, he met people of different social classes—Muslim and Christian, refugee and migrant, Senator and ordinary citizen—and always came out saying they had something good to give and something to teach him. He respected everyone.

Yet, as an American he must have felt so vulnerable, as vulnerable perhaps as we "imports" from Manila did. For what was he doing in a poverty-stricken, conflict-ridden area? He was suspect in the eyes of the Marcos regime's military men, who saw Davao as Big Trouble, and strangers as possibly aiding the dissidents. Here, they were not entirely wrong. But the centers of mass media were so distant, military men in Mindanao could assault anybody without family or friend knowing about it for some time, and the soldiers knew it, and took confidence from it.

But in the eyes of the underground resistance, Gene was not to be readily trusted either, because it was HIS government that backed the dictator. Everyone believed that without massive US military aid the regime would have fallen a long time ago. Gene must have simply laughed off the tensions and hung out with us, staff of the Mindanao Sulu Pastoral Conference Secretariat (MSCPS), then led by a charismatic lay person, Karl Gaspar. We worked extremely hard to promote justice and peace in the region and foster understanding between Christians and Muslims—communities sharply divided not by issues of faith as much as by persistent issues of land and governance. There were so many challenges, and so few short-term rewards.

We used to sing and joke around, to pray and perform liturgical rites—mainly to drown our uncertainties and gnawing fears. Here we discovered that Gene loved to sing from the depths of his belly, which showed he was calling to God as much as we were—to come and preserve us from the imagined terrors and demons beating in our hearts.

> At the CPT training in Kitchener, Ontario in the summer of 2000, Gene was there for only two days but again I was struck by his power. I remember particularly his leading of the hymn, "Wade In the Water." Never have I seen and heard such emotion put into the singing of a hymn
>
> - *Murray Lumley, Toronto, Ontario.*

To gain stability, Gene and Dorothy immersed themselves in a nearby community, and rented a one-bedroom shack in the district of Agdao, a dwelling now impossible to locate. The area has been overturned by commerce and urban high rises, and the only sign that the place ever existed is perhaps the remains of an old church, which was a hundred meters from where they dwelt. But back in 1976, it was a precious couple's home. Gene learned to squat on the wooden floor, watching the sun filter through the slats of the palo-china walls, as well as the sound of children playing in the mound under the solo mango tree. At night, he and Dorothy put their plates and utensils in a basin, and covered everything with a plastic tent to ward off the insects that invariably descended on the abodes of the poor.

Gene and author enjoy ice cream at an office party at the Mindanao Sulu Pastoral Conference Secretariat in Davao (1976)

"Simple living" was the mantra among church activists then, and the popular diet consisted of slivers of fish, root crops and vegetables cropped from the backyard. Gene and Dorothy lived by that measure, and claimed they loved the plentiful veggies, and sometimes checked on our budget to see whether their figures were still slim and closely approximated ours. (In truth, it is we who cheated, for we had relatives who took pains to subsidize us.)

But living among the urban poor, it was easy to be strict and simple. Families were truly extended, and no boundaries existed between what was public and private, open and intimate. Neighbors religiously inquired into their lives, peering through their doorway in the morning to ask why, *por dios por santo*, they still didn't have a baby. It never seemed to faze Gene, who never did anything about it till the end.

Instead, he read a lot of local literature and wrote, went on foot and recorded the many stories of people who flocked to his side and unburdened their sorrows. He immersed himself in the culture, and seemed to have fun doing as the locals did—eating on fronds and banana leaves, squeezing into jeepneys and low-ceilinged tricycles, and on All Saints Day, even going to the cemetery to celebrate the spirits of the beloved dead.

He also breezed through police checkpoints, observed how fines can disappear if police officers are handled well, and recorded these observations by practicing photography with Vir Montecastro, a remarkable guru living with family in a secluded farm.

If there were physical hardships to be borne, the greater worry of course belonged to those he sought out in his writing and research work: ethnic minorities in their harsh mountain dwellings, stevedores hungry at the wharf, farmers conned into corporate farming, banana plantation workers blistered by sun and chemical solutions, or radical pastors under interrogation and torture. He recorded them all.

Out of this effort came monographs and articles for American and Philippine magazines and journals, as well as Dorothy's first book, *Critical Choices: a Journey with the Filipino People*, a moving memoir of martial law in Davao. A solidarity group in Chicago also came out of this experience, which linked American friends to little known stories of the anti-martial law movement in the Philippines. "Synapses," formed after their return to the US, became a medium and symbol of hope for those battling injustice, and one of the many organizations that helped end US military aid to the Marcos dictatorship.

Of course, the post-Marcos era did not translate into the Paradise we thought would come to light after the "February

> **Lyrical Note**
>
> You chose to walk with us on a contrary path opposed to the powers that be.
> You were a gentle partner on that trek of difficult years.
> That phase seems over.
> But not so, the friendship forged on the way.
>
> - *Tony Ferrer, Bataan Philippines*

Revolution" and People Power of 1986. Far from it. But the 14-year experience of martial law forged deep friendships and increased the resolve to better our ways as advocates of genuine peace. Despite the terrible sacrifices exacted by the martial law era and the bleakness of its aftermath, Gene was never grim about our future. In desperate situations, he would simply say, "Well, a miracle can happen." I like to think that though we have not completely vanquished poverty, corruption and injustice in the Philippines, Gene's journey with us during those trying moments helped us immensely but also helped him in transforming his part of the world, and in his creative witnessing for global peace—reverberating as does the flutter of the wings of a butterfly, across the globe.

Whenever I met him in the US, Gene made it a point to remember only what was good in us. When General Antonio Taguba made a scathing report of the treatment of prisoners in Abu Ghraib in 2004 and accused the Bush Administration of torture and war crimes, Gene was so proud of this courageous act and sent his Filipino friends the articles detailing Taguba's ancestry, which was Filipino.

When, jetlagged and wrestling with family problems, I gave a very confused talk to a group he had gathered together in Chicago, I felt so downhearted at my failure to communicate, but he still exuded light. He placed a warm hand on my shoulder and said, "It was very helpful." Somehow, he made people feel they had wisdom, and needed to be listened to, whatever their concerns. He never felt he was exceptional, even if other Americans did. He honored diversity, and saw a myriad of possibilities within complex things, the many languages in which peace can be spoken.

It is not surprising therefore that his hopes were genuine and his sense of humor irrepressible. Because his view of the future was undimmed, he embraced the latest information technology as unhesitatingly as he recruited young people who likewise had the conviction that everyone had a part in securing peace. Over the 34 years since he first came to the Philippines, he kept in touch with his many friends and maintained relationships that were neither simply functional nor utilitarian. He visited time and time again, and in 2007 brought a 3-person CPT delegation for projects of peace and reconciliation. "A small one," he said, "to keep goals realistic." Always, during these peace missions, he took time for nurturing intimate, personal ties.

These were the friends he eagerly mobilized last year to "write a poem, a paragraph, a blessing," so they could join in spirit in the big celebration he had planned, for Dorothy's 60th birthday. These were friends to whom he gave the delicate earrings he crafted out of twigs in their home in Ontario, and friends he thanked in Dorothy's name following her trip to the Philippines to share Body Talk System therapy sessions.

In our last phone conversation, Gene said he was open to the idea of his blogged articles coming out in an anthology. But I think his best book is already out there—in the hearts of Filipinos like me who will remember him as one who journeyed with us for peace at a most difficult time, eyes filled with mirth and wonder. And always with hope. It is a book whose thread is one of risk and romance, of faith and struggle, and of the perfect balancing of the yin and yang. Gene was our Exceptional American.

DREAMS AND PEACEMAKING: PHILIPPINES

December 28, 2005

G*ene read all of Carl Jung's writings during his time in Washington, DC in the late 1960s immediately following his stint in Vietnam. His respect for the power of dreams opened doors for him in many cultures.*

Dreams are a portal into people's lives. And they do reflect our internal conflicts and unresolved problems, what an earlier era may have referred to as demon inspired impulses, pieces of unconnected or unresolved energy and instinct.

When Dorothy and I worked in the Philippines in the late 1970s we were invited by church workers to go into the T'boli tribal area in the mountains of Southern Mindanao. The Asia Development Bank and the Philippine government through its indigenous directorate had decided to construct a major dam to create electricity in the homeland of these people. Most of the tribal people were terrified at the thought of the dam because it would destroy their villages and life as they knew it. We were guests of the local Sta. Cruz Mission and our task was to talk to local people and help figure out a way to tell the story we heard. We spent a total of about a month in the area and we began work by going around to community people and their chiefs called Datus. We did not speak the local dialect so we worked through interpreters. This made us uncomfortable but it was the only way to proceed.

The first step was to win the villagers' confidence so that they would talk to us honestly and forthrightly. They had every reason to suspect us as agents of international finance. Introductions by local church workers, community leaders, and trusted companions were crucial in the process.

Early on in our visits people began to hint at terrible dreams they were having, so we thought we would invite them to tell us their dreams as part of the survey. Both of us had studied anthropology and I, having already moved through my love affair with dreams, recognized their importance. The more the people recognized our openness to hearing their dreams the more we tried to create space for them to talk about them without presuming to probe unfairly. Their dreams indicated impending doom. Our willingness to listen to these vivid pictures of what they thought would happen to their beautiful valley created rapport between us and people began to line up wanting to talk. We now believe that our openness to their horrific dreams helped develop a bond and inspired us on a deeper level to work diligently to carry out the piece of the protest to the dam that they were not equipped to carry out.

Midway through our work our non T'boli hosts and sponsors invited us to reflect on how we were doing. We communicated enthusiasm and excitement. Our discussion ranged over various matters and finally settled on one final and pressing question. "We think this is going pretty well," said our sponsors, "but we keep hearing from the people that you are talking to them about their dreams and we can't understand what this has to do with the problem of the dam."

We left still convinced that dreams could be one of various parts of the development of a campaign to stop the dam. We wrote our report and did a slide show which was distributed widely to schools and churches in the surrounding lowland areas. Before any of this material was released, we went back and invited local feedback. The T'boli people were overjoyed that we had listened to their horrible dreams and the non T'boli sponsors conceded that this might have been helpful. Eventually our work became part of a larger organizing effort in the region of Mindanao and the dam was never built. Our engagement with the deeper psychic energy of the T'boli people was a key factor in the success of this effort. The title of our slide show, *Where will we hang the light bulbs?* came from a line the T'boli people themselves shared in one of our animated discussions, "Where will we hang the light bulbs? In the trees? Our houses will be flooded by the dam." The title introduced a sense of urgency and mystery to a story that on the surface pitted modern development against traditional values and life.

My own experience with dreams encourages me to be more open to their messages for our work of nonviolence and wholeness, not just as individuals but as communities. I believe that people who invite dream discussion in sensitive situations where violence is rampant should have experienced the importance of dreams in their own lives. Finally, my experience suggests that being alert to dreams, within ourselves and others, provides access to unexpected waves of energy and spiritual unity that even the best organizing cannot accomplish.

PHILIPPINES: MIGRANT WORKERS

January 4, 2007

On New Year's night when I arrive at the airport in Manila, I notice signs welcoming the return of Filipino workers from around the world. I see them at my side searching the baggage claim area for their heavy suitcases crammed with gifts for family, friends, and maybe even for the Mayor of their distant barrios. When they reach their homes there will be tears of happiness mixed with the pain of lonely times abroad. Now for a few days they will be dignitaries, much loved for their sacrifice on behalf of the people who gave them life.

One in ten Filipinos work abroad, often under testy and lonely conditions. Some of the migrant workers waiting at the baggage claim may not have received all of their $200 per month salaries due to misunderstandings or dishonest employers. Still, they continue to travel to countries stretching from Southeast Asia to the Middle East, Europe and the Americas where they work sometimes seven days a week to bring home a tiny sum for the people they love. As I watch their eyes searching for luggage, I think of the Mexican workers in Chicago and the vegetable estates or construction sites all over my own country. My mind sees a nation of hands stretching for survival above and below the radar of regulations.

The long days of Filipino and Mexican workers in fields, construction sites, and homes remind me of my youth when I did that kind of work. In those days I was ignorant of how my skin color carried privilege. As a college student I worked beside Mexican workers at the packing plant. They worked hard and were more adept and faster on the poultry line. One day during my tenure as a college student at Goshen College in Indiana I found out that my co-workers on the line earned much less than I did. I remember the sense of confusion that discovery awakened within me. I had no framework for understanding. At first I thought my extra pay must be some kind of generosity directed to students like me striving to meet their tuition. One day I discovered the huts—maybe old chicken houses—where my co-workers lived.

The memory of their worn and scarred hands has stayed with me for 45 years. They taught me the basics of the international worker system and over time I learned bit by bit how privilege, charity, and oppression support one another.

The migrant workers survive at the boundary of full citizenship where hope, anger, and resignation mix with occasional opportunities for escape to a fuller life. It is a scary territory where employers fear organized migrants, and migrants learn to expand every opportunity in order to avoid consignment to that distant village where economic hope has lost its way.

The signs at the Manila airport shout at me WELCOME HOME. But I am not home. I now come from a world that has forgotten how to dig ditches, harvest with hands, and perform hard manual labor. I live in a world where work is defined by words, computers, and communication. The people who invite me to dinner struggle with being overweight or talk about vacation plans to distant sites of ancient treasure.

I am a person who was given the gift of hope and I did go on to a life of organizing, of trying to be an ally to workers. But what should I do about my doubt? I feel awkward because it is taking me so long to integrate into daily life some very simple lessons that began many years ago on the poultry line. I grew up in a time when we talked of civil rights. I now grow old in a time of migrant rights. And I know there are miles to go to WELCOME HOME the nation of migrant workers so deserving of hope.

RECOVERING FROM THIS AGE OF TOXICITY: A NOTE TO IRAQ FROM THE PHILIPPINES

January 23, 2007

Dear Friends in Iraq,

News of increased troop levels and warfare in your land has reached us. My travels here in the Philippines took me for brief tours of former American military bases that were once the forward logistical supply routes for the wars in this part of Asia. Although it has been many months since I was with you in Baghdad where I listened to the stories of detainees, I have a clear image of the increased burden of violence now upon you. I imagine with horror the columns of military vehicles weaving their way in narrow streets where homes and storefronts of your neighborhoods abound. As I write I remember vividly my conversations with medical professionals and citizens in Iraq about another toxic product of the modern warfare, depleted uranium, arising from the use of ammunition shells.

Last week I walked among the deserted and deteriorating concrete magazines in the US bases at Subic and Clark where ammunition bound for a war front, was once stored. The grass growing above these empty hulls, planted there decades ago to disguise the magazine's purpose is now deepening its roots and will someday overcome the concrete and iron roofs. I thought of you, especially the families, friends and religious leaders who support the thousands of detainees in your land. I thought of the great volumes of explosive material that have been expended in Iraq.

I wish you could have been with me when I met Mr. Dino, 76, who carries in his body the imprint of his long years of work at Subic Naval Base. Mr. Dino's humor is infectious as he describes moving ammunition shipments about the vast storage area. As he tells his story I learn that his body is heavily infected with asbestos, a construction material now long known to be dangerous. When the war of Southeast Asia waned he was rotated out of the magazine to another construction and maintenance site on the Subic Naval Base. He is one of 1000 former base workers in his town whose condition, asbestos poisoning in the lungs, has been confirmed by medical tests. Some of his colleagues have died, and many will have their lives cut short by the infection in their bodies.

Gene interviews Mr. Dino, accompanied by Teofilo "Boojie" Juatco of the Alliance for Bases Clean-up in Olongapo, Philippines (2008)

Mr. Dino took me to meet three of his friends who suffer similar afflictions. Carlos Marta, 59, was sleeping in his chair under a metal roof shade when we arrived. His wife awakened him. With labored breathing Carlos struggled to join our conversation, his body visibly in pain. His condition has worsened markedly in the last six months. Carlos and two other colleagues described the difficulty they have experienced in getting medical help from either their former American employers or the Philippine government. Neither government wants to assume responsibility or liability. As I listened to their stories I saw you beside them reaching out for a fair measure of time in life.

At the former Clark Air Force Base, a facility once the size of the nation of Singapore now being transformed into a development zone, I met several women who described miscarriages, persistent headaches, and other symptoms related to residual discarded military waste that has not been properly cleaned up at the former base and in communities that border the base. Heroic efforts to identify the problems have been carried out by local groups including the Task Force on Bases Clean Up spearheaded by our long time activist friend, Myrla Baldonado.

The former US bases here are monuments to the toxicity of modern warfare. I hope that even in the midst of your darkest hours in Iraq you might have the opportunity of sending an official or unofficial delegation here to the Philippines to visit these abandoned military facilities so that grass roots victims here can show you how firm and vigilant you have to be in dealing with nations who install foreign bases in your country. What has been learned here is that the toxic damage is carried in the bodies and the surrounding environment for generations and leads to early death and enormous pain in the earth, in the animals, the vegetation, and among people. I know that you will someday be left alone to recover from the nightmare that you are now going through. Long after the final explosions some of you, my Iraqi friends, will be left with the lonely task of cleaning up the consequences of war.

I am very much aware that depleted uranium, one newer strand of toxic material, has accompanied your war. Your medical doctors and citizens have experienced and documented this weapon's potential for mass destruction for almost a generation. I know that American authorities have taken no responsibility for this new plague of toxicity. Your willingness to speak out will be a gift for humanity everywhere and a special contribution to a world inviting moral leadership. Thank you for the sacrifice and risk you will carry as you assume this additional burden. Be assured that many of us will share in the hard work of scientific research and agitation to alert the world to the price that will inevitably be paid to restore our earth. We hope our work together might install a binding legal mechanism that will prevent this scourge from being visited on future generations.

Sincerely,

Gene Stoltzfus

From 1962-1971, approximately 18 million gallons of Agent Orange were sprayed on millions of acres in Vietnam to destroy jungles so that enemy forces could be identified, and to eradicate crops that might have been supporting them. According to the Vietnamese Ministry of Foreign Affairs, Operation Ranch Hand, code name for the Agent Orange project, an estimated 400,000 Vietnamese have died or been disabled from defoliants, primarily Agent Orange. Another 500,000 children have been born with birth defects.

A role play at a high school in Wetzlar, Germany (2009). Gene shares how CPT teams work to de-escalate crisis in militarized situations.

Gene and soldier at health dispensary in Vietnam (1964)

On a return trip in 2009 he befuddles a Vietnamese fruit vendor in Hanoi

THE IMPACT OF WAR ON POVERTY

Speech presented at a Micah Challenge Conference held in Edmonton, Alberta on June 22-23, 2007

Micah Challenge (*www.micahchallenge.org*) *is a worldwide initiative among evangelical Christians from poorer nations to awaken people to the work of overcoming poverty, engaging in development, and doing justice. The conference reminded participants that the 15-year time frame of the Challenge, which began in 2000, was half completed and much remains to be done.*

Micah 6:8, "What does the LORD require of you? To do justice, and to love kindness, and to walk humbly with your God."

Conviction arising from faith is the home base out of which I have worked for the past 44 years—ever since I went to Vietnam as a civilian volunteer and development worker. My time in Vietnam changed my life. I experienced massive destruction and lost friends, both American and Vietnamese, and was challenged to reconstruct my entire understanding of spiritual life and of the work of people of faith. I was pressed into activism and into a deeper understanding of who God is.

In Vietnam I saw soldiers being asked to die for a nation or for a politic that they may, or may not, have believed in. I asked myself, would people like me have the discipline to organize ourselves, the patience to train ourselves, and the courage to engage ourselves to do the things that make for peace, just as soldiers were asked to do every day, risking their lives to defeat the enemy? And I asked, what would be required to develop a culture of peace and peacemaking that might change the entire violent paradigm of conflict and reconciliation that has dominated world affairs for at least 5,000 years. These are the questions I have worked with for 44 years.

What should I say about war and poverty? Should I marshal statistics? Tell stories? Or, should I dig deeper to try to identify trends or little slices of what seems like truth along the way? People have called me an activist, even though I spring from seven generations of Mennonite pastors and still see myself in that line. The role of the activist organizer is to make coherent the connections between poverty and violence, creating a pathway so people can understand the connections and do something about them. Long after I decided to work to end the Vietnam war, and then to continue working on the problem of war as my life's work, I discovered that I was part of a great religious and activist tradition reaching back through the prophets, Jesus, St. Francis, and various social and labor movements.

Friends and teachers now long gone, at least in the template of time as we understand it, have continued to cheer me on in the work: Tommy Douglas, Dorothy Day, Louis Riel, Eugene Debs, Jane Addams, Rosa Parks, and Charles Finney. These are but a few of the names in this great cloud of witnesses—whose persistence through both victories and crushing defeats has inspired me in this work. Their distinguishing characteristic is that they were part of a group that trained, supported each other, and disciplined themselves for a life that points the way to justice. Another thread that has connected these activists to me has been their search to find a safe place in their hearts where the divine spirit had space, and where transcendent meaning for the whole universe was at home, even among the stresses and the impossible odds.

I had a dream one night last week. In the dream, I was in Cambodia as part of a team to evaluate a development project. The Cambodia of the dream was not like the one I visited in 1963—lush with fruit, gardens, forests, and rice fields. No, in my dream, as far as I could see, there was hardly a tree. Far

in the distance I could see Angkor Wat, 12th century wonder of the world, built as an act of worship by Brahman and Buddhist imperial rulers. But in my dream Angkor Wat showed many signs of damage from 20th century warfare. Looking to the southwest in my dream, I saw what was left of the modern-day Cambodian monarchy's palaces, also heavily damaged by war. Much of the once heavily populated countryside in the area was depopulated due to bombs and genocide. Shrubs and grass had now taken over where lush green rice paddies had fed a population for centuries. Our small delegation began to search for the development project. For a time we thought we had come to the wrong country, or at least the wrong place in Cambodia.

But we were stuck because we had no transportation. In the medium distance I saw the shell of an old, partially destroyed concrete building. Drab, naked pillars, some pock marked with bullet holes, told its story. It could have been the product of some great project of one of the political/ development experiments that overcame Cambodia in the last 50 years: French imperialism, Prince Sihanouk after independence (the last of the Cambodian royalty), Lon Nol (a project of American neo-colonialism), Pol Pot and fundamentalist utopian communism, Vietnamese liberationists, or today's "back-to-normal" democracy. Our small delegation made its way to the massive dilapidated concrete structure where we found the office of the small development project that was helping local people plant vegetables. I felt confused about this part of the dream. I don't know a lot about vegetables, except that it is good to eat them. The project managers seemed a little nervous about our visit, knowing that if our delegation did not give them a good report, outside support would be terminated.

This dream was given to me for the benefit of all of us. Each of us will see different threads in the dream that make us feel embarrassed, angry, guilty or hopeless. The dream reminds us of the power that wealth, ideology, and theology have over the survival of whole civilizations. Will the next century be any better for Cambodia, for all of us? Or is the present tiny development project in that country just a recess, while great forces conspire to put forward another experiment of "development" through the barrel of a gun? Can humanity and the earth survive this period through which we are passing? Is there a good thing left to do? Now, that is a very practical and spiritual question. Is there hope, and a pathway to live out that hope? Here the interconnection of spirit and action is not just a luxury—it is a matter of life and death.

During my trips to Iraq in the first two years of the American-led occupation I often met soldiers and their commanders. Many of them sincerely wanted to do good. As Christian Peacemakers we needed to be in touch with them to keep human rights matters in the forefront of their minds. Often they would say to us, "We are just here to help the Iraqis help themselves. And we will get out when our job is done." My eyes would glaze over when I heard those lines, the same words I heard in Vietnam and elsewhere. That mindset didn't work very well there and it doesn't seem to work in Iraq either. I remained friendly to the soldiers while masking my deeply felt ambivalence.

But my point is not to blame the military and its political/industrial support structures for the smart bombs they introduce in Iraq and Afghanistan. The military is part of *us*. *We* pay for these weapons with our tax dollars. This makes visible who we are, our addictions to consulting, advising, and schemes that "make things come out right." It reminds us how hard it is to listen to people, especially poor people, to communicate heart-to-heart. It reminds us to carry our projects and schemes lightly, with convictions that are deeply informed by local people. We really like to use the language of empowerment that our politicians and economists teach us. And we sort-of believe that "If you give a person a fish they can eat for a day, but if you teach a person to fish they can eat for a lifetime." We like to believe that the reason First Nations people have such a hard life is that they don't know how to do anything but fish and scrounge in the forest for food, and that the government programs are lousy. Sometimes they are lousy. But those government programs are us too. They express our convictions about fishing and forests and food. And about the accumulation of wealth.

Poverty and war! In Colombia, our Christian Peacemaker Teams group often worked with villages along the Opon River. The villagers had become refugees because several competing underground and national armies wanted to control their area and by extension gain access to a lucrative gas pipeline. The gas was waiting to be stolen to support someone's revolutionary program, paramilitary mob, or military. By showing up there in canoes on a regular basis—foreigners and Colombians together—we were able to help create a bit of security. Most of the people came back to their villages, but not without the price of assassinations.

Now these folks did not need to learn to read, cook, fish, plant vegetables, or engage in micro-business enterprises. They were not university graduates, but by and large the Opon people could do all of these things probably as well as or better than university graduates. What they really needed was for armed groups, official and unofficial, to get off their backs for good. Last week there was an engagement between the Colombian armed forces and the FMLN, one of two revolutionary armies in that area. The firefight could be heard by the Opon villagers, and several soldiers were killed. This is very bad news for the villages.

In parts of the world like Iraq, security contractors, our modern-day mercenaries, are known to earn upwards of $1,000 per day. The soldiers who did the fighting last week in Opon earn about $200 per month and a cell phone, about the same as an elementary school teacher. You do the math to figure out other things that could be done in the Opon villages if the money went to people and not to war. If you were an undereducated villager and soldiering was offered to you at $200 dollars per month, and your other choice was unemployment with a dismal, landless future, what would you do? Even if your friends and family didn't like the idea of you being a soldier? And if you are a former soldier trained in the ways of weapons, it is equally difficult for you to turn down generous Pentagon incentives to join the war efforts in Iraq and Afghanistan.

In Colombia many warriors have cell phones. We learned in our work that we could contact them for dialogue. The fighters on all sides believe that if their group can win, they will bring in real development and the people will be happy. They believe that after the final battle the guy at the top will be toppled and the road to the good life is open. Some form of this thinking is present with all the factions. Another form of this is present in most of us too.

Come to think of it, their language is not a whole lot different than the publicity around Canadian forces in Afghanistan they don't even presume to wait until the reason for last battle is won. They are there to bring security and development at the same time. Many Canadians also believe their military can do appropriate and real development with a rifle in one hand and vegetable seeds, paint, and hammer, in the other. Maybe they can. But in Afghanistan, no outside invader since Alexander the Great in the 4th century B.C. has had a lot of success making things come out their way.

In modern times both the British and Soviets were rebuked by Afghan forces. After 9/11 Al Qaeda was ecstatic because the Americans and their supporters were now coming to Afghanistan and this would provide another opportunity for them to spread multinational Islamic jihad. I notice that things aren't going really well for the Canadian Forces. Maybe it is time to resurrect and improve upon Canada's four decades of historic peacekeeping in the world. If Canadian development and poverty workers want to set a real, identifiable goal for the next ten years, how about this as a top priority: the complete elimination of the Canadian Armed Forces as a fighting force

Vietnam (1964)

and its transformation into an unarmed premier peacemaking body to be called upon by the nations of the world.

One of the things we did in refugee communities and poor areas in Vietnam was to distribute appropriate vegetable seeds and cuttings. Sometimes I took those seeds along to give to people, always hoping they wouldn't ask me too many technical questions that I could not answer. Over time, some of our volunteers learned that a specific type of sweet potato did very well, so when we had sweet potato cuttings we often took them into the countryside. Even I could understand the technical details of sweet potatoes. Just plant the cuttings and give them a little water once in a while. Hallelujah! In a few months there will be big, healthy, tasty sweet potatoes. That worked for a while, but of course as the war expanded people were forced off the land and the sweet potatoes rotted in the soil.

As the war progressed we got more involved with human rights. One of our projects was to try to bring the tiger cages to the attention of the world. The tiger cages were part of a special prison on an island off the coast in the South China Sea. The cages were at ground level and people were thrown into the pits below, some for months at a time. Sometimes, to overcome the smell, lime was thrown on the prisoners. On several occasions we tried to take congressional people or journalists to see the tiger cages. We could gain access to the prison but never to the tiger cage area.

On one occasion several congresspersons agreed to accompany a colleague who once did a lot of work with sweet potatoes. During the carefully crafted tour over manicured prison facilities, the visitors came upon a small sweet potato patch. My friend Don Luce initiated a conversation with the prison officials about sweet potatoes. The guards behind the hidden door got curious. They wanted to meet this foreigner who actually spoke Vietnamese and was interested in sweet potatoes. Suddenly the secret and hidden door to the tiger cages was flung open and photographers, congresspersons, and volunteers poured into the tiger cage area, to the consternation of the prison warden. Pictures of that encounter spread around

> From the first time I heard Gene speak Vietnamese in 1966 I said to myself I wanted to be like him so I could have fun the way he was having fun, communicating with the people.
> - *Tom Fox*, *National Catholic Reporter, Kansas City.*

the world and helped end the war. But remember, it was the humble sweet potato that opened the door.

Our goals for development, which include the transfer of resources to areas of poverty, carry hope when they do not come out of the barrel of a gun. Militarism, gangs, and warlords are pushing us in the opposite direction. If we are going to stop terrorism we need to stop being terrorists ourselves.

In the dream I shared earlier, I noticed that the project was to plant vegetables in that barren, war-ravaged land of Cambodia. In the dream the wars were over. The B-52s had gone home, their role in future wars gradually subsumed by smart bombs and missiles. Only the carnage of concrete buildings remained, along with the tiny plots of vegetables. But are the tiny plots enough to pronounce the development project a success? One of those vegetables was probably sweet potatoes, the same species that opened the prison doors of the tiger cages so that the prisoners, and the world, could breathe. In the dream I felt trapped. There was no place to seal myself off from the devastation that lingered. Neither the Twin Towers nor the gated communities of advanced capitalism are secure. So how am I going to evaluate this development project? What is success? A few plants have survived the battle. People, albeit with wounds, have survived. At some level my dream engine wanted to find a way out. But there was no way out. I felt like the prophet Ezekiel when he was placed in the valley of dry bones: "Our bones are dried up and our hope is lost. We are clean cut off (Ezekiel 37:11)." And then the dream engine talked to me, saying that out of the dry bones and the bomb craters, breath will enter and there will be life.

The dream did not explicitly show other effects of war, such as psychological dysfunction (PTSD) and its cousin, the destruction of culture and community. Many of us may have failed to notice that the process of war-making in the Cambodias of this world brings in its wake spiritual nihilism or absolutism, and replaces wisdom with fundamentalism. My dream occurred long after the real battles in Cambodia and did not explicitly draw my attention to criminals, opportunism, and corruption—all of which reach disgusting depths of demented illegal and legal behavior. There is not a village that does not have stories and multiple patterns that tell about loss of family and neighbor, loss of property and possessions, loss of respect and human dignity.

Activists, scholars, prayer warriors, record keepers, artists, and money people—we are all needed in this work. Have we made any progress at all? We are invited to look behind the record of humanity's most violent century to see the massive social changes that have happened nonviolently. From India to Eastern Europe, from democratic movements in China to freedom walks in the USA, from little-known villages in Afghanistan, to farmers and fisher folk in Colombia, people have discovered the power of nonviolent action, a power deeply rooted in the gospel. These signs of hope never come without imperfection because we are human. Some of us are overcoming our guilt, hopelessness, and individualism. The air might be clearing as we grow one step at a time, acting, reflecting, leaning, stumbling, practicing, training, then moving forward again. The promise of that old South African freedom song now adopted by the peace movement is with us, "We shall not give up the fight, we have only started, we have only started, we have only started. Together we'll have victory hand holding hand."

Why do I close on this note of hope? I have led many delegations to desperately poor and violence-infested areas. In some places there is silence because of fear—fear that visitors like me might be connected to some military or security program like the CIA. But in most places, the startling impression one gets is of people engaged, seeking to move forward. When I ask delegates to evaluate their experience, often the first word to come from their mouths is—hope. Often they say, "I came to learn, but I leave with hope." Hope comes when people do something concrete about their situation, when they work together, when they train themselves for the next step, when they pray together, and then when they act. Hope is the renewable fuel that gives us power to reach beyond the boundaries of past centuries and paradigms. Hope gives us courage to build alliances with people we once saw as enemies or war victims, but with whom we now can become partners in a great global 21st century experiment of organizing for peace.

HAITI PEACE CHOIR

December 27, 2005

Once during a trip to Haiti, our plans were completely stalled by one of the many moments of crisis and violence that consumed Haiti in the 1990s. We walked downtown to Port-au-Prince's Iron Market to get a feel for what was happening. I was more than a little worried about everyone's security because we clearly stood out as foreigners and there was much anger in the air, to say nothing of the reality of death squads and a police-military establishment that ran the country by terror. I saw in some of the faces the seeds of mob action, but also the marvelous possibilities for transformation.

As we emerged from the market, I knew what we needed. We needed to sing. We needed a peace choir, right there on the street corner of the Iron Market, to break the silence of fear and repression with crisp notes of hope. We sang "We are Marching in the Light of God" for the very first time when we were on the bus in Haiti. The words and music baptized all of us and gave a tiny break from the heavy killing that was going on around us. In Haiti, I first realized that we had found one of the songs that would keep us moving together in life and death.

GETTING IN THE WAY

December 10, 2007

In the early days of Christian Peacemaker Teams we wanted to find a simple phrase that could represent our experiment in peacemaking. We expected that somewhere in our engagement with the broken stuff of our world, a phrase growing directly from experience would become apparent to all of us. Eleven years after the vision for teams of Christian Peacemakers was first articulated at a Mennonite World Conference, and seven years after we began program work, the result of our quest began to make itself known. The answer was simple, engaging and connected to a long religious and spiritual history. When we found it, there was no further debate. It seemed so right —"Getting in the Way."

The year was 1995. The place was Hebron in the Palestinian West Bank. A major massacre of Palestinians had occurred at a site important to Jews and Muslims, a site where Abraham and Sarah are entombed. In response to the mayor's invitation and the advice of local people, a CPT project began. All of us in CPT were finding our way, testing methods to act, and to prevent violence. We knew, for example, that Israeli settlers threatened Palestinian school children and we began to look for ways to be with them in a presence of protection.

On November 4, CPTer Wendy Lehman and a new delegation participant, Dianne Roe, went out to accompany children at the Cordoba Elementary School. As Dianne stood talking to some teenage girls, several settlers pushed her to the ground and kicked her. The settler youth also attacked the students, dragging them by their hair. Twenty minutes later a settler armed with an Uzi threatened Wendy, Dianne, and other CPTers. On the same afternoon, 80 settlers blocked the road where students walked to and from their school. November 4 was a tumultuous day. That same evening an Israeli militant from Hebron shot and killed Israeli Prime Minister Yitzhak Rabin in Tel Aviv.

The following week Dianne was back in Corning, New York, reporting to her home church when a woman in her congregation asked, "Why didn't you just get out of the way so you wouldn't be hurt?" The option had never occurred to Dianne. In violence reduction you don't just get out of the way whenever your personal safety is threatened.

Sometime later Dianne was invited to create a banner for an international conference organized by Sabeel, a Palestinian Christian peace organization. The conference organizers wanted to incorporate the notion of Way, an early name for Christians. The main feature of the banner was feet in worn sandals. Dianne used a photograph of Wendy's feet as a model. The feet of CPTer Sister Anne Montgomery also contributed to the final banner. After an animated discussion, the phrase, GETTING IN THE WAY, was superimposed on the feet.

The Way (Acts 9:2) is a word that appears frequently in the New Testament and is actually part of the grounding of other world religions. In Islam, Sharia law hints at the notion of a Way. Buddhism speaks of the Middle Way, a path of moderation between the extremes of asceticism and sensual indulgence. I inquired at Sabeel for permission to use

Gene was the leader with a vision for preserving the dignity of all human beings especially in areas of conflict. He inspired so many of us to walk "on" and "in" the way of Jesus Christ, serving with love and working for a just peace and reconciliation.

- *Nora Carmi, Coordinator, Community Building and Women's Programs, Sabeel Ecumenical Liberation Theology Center, Jerusalem* the banner drawing and the phrase. They agreed, and we began to test out our signature phrase, "Getting in the Way."

My primary conviction for rooting ourselves in the basic language of Way was that it reaches to the foundational threads of Christianity, to stories of Jesus himself and his followers who combined healing, confrontation, public discourse, suffering, and possible death at the personal and political level, all as an inherent part of the journey. This is a perfect place from which to launch the project of violence reduction.

Getting in the Way implies that there is a way. It's a way that requires healthy feet and clear convictions nurtured in the spirit; it leads through villages and cities, across oceans, mountains, and rivers. It incorporates a persistent spirit that is not seduced by the twin diversions of compulsive activism or unengaged living.

Spirit of the Way suggests that the person on the pathway will not easily veer off course or look backward, tempted by power, wealth or security. The Way knows that in the real world people will encounter words, individuals, and systems that can pull them off the path— "benign" racist statements, little lies, killing of innocents and non-innocents, organized violence, hatred, destruction of nature. People learn to use their minds to develop careful strategies. Their bodies are engaged and their spirits linked with the power of God throughout the whole universe.

Getting in the Way implies a quality of collective work and decision making that still retains flexibility for an individuality that is not bound by short-term ego needs. This way has unexpected

> ### GETTING OUT OF THE WAY
>
> As Christian Peacemaker Teams (CPT) welcomed more members from outside the US and Canada, and began looking through an anti-racist lens in a more intentional way, we were made aware of problems with the "Getting in the Way" motto and imagery. Colombian CPTers said it does not translate into Spanish in a meaningful way. Also white feet can conjure up a picture of the outsider peace hero boldly confronting the powers on behalf of powerless people of color. Local partners have told us that sometimes the best thing CPT can do is get OUT of the way. Gene's vision of CPT always included supporting the efforts of local peacemakers, who at great risk to themselves, persist in mobilizing for justice. CPT is in the process of finding an image and a motto that underline that role of "accompanying" and "working alongside."
>
> *- Claire Evans, Delegation Coordinator, Christian Peacemaker Teams, December, 2010*

opportunities for transformation as well as occasional impediments and obstacles.

People of this Way are not looking to be saved by the power of the nation state and its military. In a press release about the settler attacks in 1995, Wendy Lehman summed up the components of Getting in the Way as they came to her that day in Hebron, "I've certainly learned a lot about the power of prayer and its interconnectedness with action. Our work here involves risk, and we sometimes put ourselves in situations where we have only our faith in God, the power of nonviolence, each other, and our Hebron hosts to keep us safe. Without the prayer support of our friends back home, I'm not sure we could do it."

People in the Way practice a mellow long-term militancy that is keen to read the signs of the times. Whether the message is joyful or ominous we invoke the power of God in celebration.

HEBRON DREAMS

December 28, 2005

My visit to the CPT team in Hebron in the late 1990s came at a time when the press of Israeli occupation was heavy but defused and it was hard to consolidate our efforts into one single focus.

One day our team received trustworthy information that a Palestinian youth had been killed by a grenade near the border between Israel and the West Bank. Although this area was fairly distant from the city of Hebron in the Southeast border, and not one where we had a lot of carefully developed relationships, we decided to visit the village. A Palestinian companion joined us. When we arrived at the village we were directed to the family of the victim and were welcomed into the meeting room where males gather. As we sipped tea the father told us the heart rending story of their son, an exceptionally talented and intelligent youth of 12, who had been playing in an area that looked out over a beautiful valley. Earlier, soldiers had passed through and dropped a grenade.

Tears flowed as the story was told and we recognized that this was not a time to engineer a campaign but to solemnize as Christians the mystery of this event; it was a deeply human and pastoral moment. So we asked the family if it would be OK with them if the three of us would go to the place of the child's death and pray. We knew we might be taking a risk that could backfire. They were enthusiastic, and led us immediately to the site where we knelt down to pray. Even as we prayed for God's comfort and intervention, we knew that our action still might cross some line of unacceptability. To accommodate their experience of prayer we prayed out loud and when we completed our prayer we stood and looked in silence over the valley.

We were ushered back into the house for more hospitality and sweets, and when seated, we inquired about the son who was killed. Over more tea the family which had now been joined by other members of the neighborhood talked openly about this special child, his personality and interests. At one point I hinted that this might bring new and important dreams to their lives. I knew that Muslims hold dreams in high regard since the Koran and much of the Prophet Mohammed's revelation and key life decisions had been informed by dreams.

The father was pleased to open this area of companionship and told us a dream his son had had, just days before his death. In his dream the son went to the village cemetery. He carried something that represented a treasure and he placed it in the cemetery. The child found the dream to be calming because of the treasure. The following day, he told his family this dream and wondered if they thought it had a special meaning. The family and the villagers now found great comfort in the dream and expressed thankfulness that we had come. As we left, the males kissed each other on the cheek as is the custom and in that moment we felt a sense of mystery and solidarity that we could never have anticipated.

Perhaps our visit brought some comfort to the family but certainly our actions and the child's dream empowered us to deepen our work and to overcome our fears of deeper spiritual bonding with a population deeply traumatized by violence.

> Gene will be missed by all of us specially here in occupied Palestine where he spent a lot of time trying to get justice and peace. He has left great memories here in Palestine through all the efforts of the CPT and all the work he had helped organize. We will continue his message and efforts to bring a just peace for the world. Salaam and Peace from Jerusalem.
>
> - *George S. Rishmawi, Coordinator, Siraj, Center For Holy Land Studies, Beit Sahour*

CHIAPAS DREAMS

December 28, 2005

CPT was invited to place a team in Chiapas, Mexico, where a full scale rebellion by native people was gathering momentum, resulting in the militarization of the area. Government, big ranchers, and industrialists required this land in order to harness the enormous resources of the mountains and forests. As is our style we listened to people for a time in order to develop a clear and specific focus. The larger protest movement was coordinated by a revolutionary movement that combined both nonviolent and violent means of struggle. Throughout Chiapas there were various groups who had chosen not to embrace the violent struggle. These groups included the Tzotzil people, who lived some two hours from the key city, San Cristobal. They had formed themselves into a religious community of some 20,000 people called Las Abejas (the Bees) and identified themselves as Christian pacifists. Most of them lived in difficult refugee settings and dreamed of the time when they could return to their small coffee farms. They maintained contact with the larger revolutionary group but did not join. They were heavily pressured to cooperate with government initiatives but they refused to accept any kind of aid or assistance from the vast military pacification efforts of the area. We supported them in their marches and actions. More than 40 of their people were massacred during prayer, shortly after the beginning of the general uprising of the area.

In CPT we had learned that the period of Lent was a special season of prayer, fasting and awakening of the world wide church to the victims of imperial policies of our time. This year we decided to join with Las Abejas in a Lenten fast in front of a major Mexican army civic action base. It is the custom of Las Abejas people to pray and fast and at such times they pray on their knees every four hours around the clock. Our team built a tent at the bottom of a hillside in front of the military base and several hundred yards from one of the main refugee areas. Day and night every four hours for six weeks community people and CPTers gathered in a circle to pray for justice, reconciliation, and freedom from the captivity of the refugee camp. Local people and CPTers alternated days or weeks when they engaged in full fasts. I went to visit for the final two weeks of Lent which culminated

Gene presents peace banner on the grounds of the military base outside X'oyep, Mexico (2000). Banner was used during the Tent for Lent encampment with Las Abejas community.

in a great festival gathering of Bees from the surrounding region on the Saturday before Easter. Although we helped in the processes the entire event was organized locally. We were there as international eyes, ears, and support from the churches of the world. The nights were cold and the 4:00 am prayer was a challenge for all of us.

On the first day of my visit the Morning Prayer time brought about 25 people from the village including some of the leadership. Although I had virtually no Spanish I quickly found a fluent CPTer and sat down to talk and listen to their story. As we sat, military people came and went with apparently very official looking things to do. Occasionally, young soldiers would come by and we gave them treats. Our conversations grew deeper. I asked Las Abejas if they had any warnings that this terrible exodus from their home villages would be forced on them. "Yes," they said, "we were afraid when we started to see the soldiers." So I asked, "How did you notice your fears? Did you have visits from strangers? Were you attacked? Did you have dreams?"

Immediately they described dreams of the forest burning all around them and the destruction of their villages. The emotion and power of the communication increased as they told me of their horrible dreams. Then

Gene with military commander at the base outside X'oyep, in Chiapas, Mexico (2000)

I asked about local traditions concerning dreams. They said, "We take our dreams very seriously and important dreams like this are taken first to our families where we talk about them and then to our elders who also talk about them in the village." Their dreams warned them about what was coming and they seemed relieved to be able to share this part of their lives.

Las Abejas were marked people. They were tough but had become aware of the enormous changes that threatened their existence. They called upon the constellation of spiritual resources available in traditional and contemporary practices like the Lenten fast and their dream life to give them sustaining energy and power to persevere.

THE JAPANESE PEACE CONSTITUTION

From a letter sent July 10, 2005

This morning I spoke to 1000 high school students here in Sapporo, Japan, my eleventh presentation in universities, churches and other settings. My visit to Japan was facilitated by Yorifumi Yaguchi, visionary Japanese peace leader, poet and professor. We were classmates at Goshen College in the late 1950's.

I tried to demonstrate in front of students and through an interpreter how to get in the way of soldiers in Palestine. The principal said that all the teachers will now be discussing CPT in their classes. I closed the speech with a call for the students to remember the country's secret but most important export: the Japanese constitution.

This evening my colleague Sister Anne Montgomery and I will be meeting with Japanese lawyers who are preparing a lawsuit against the Japanese Government's decision to send the Japanese self-defense force to Iraq. It's very controversial and Japanese citizens feel that there is much pressure from both inside the country and from abroad to change their pacifist constitution.

Article 9 of the Japanese constitution says, "Aspiring sincerely to an international peace based on justice and order, the Japanese people forever renounce war as a sovereign right of the nation and the threat of use of force as a means of settling international disputes. In order to accomplish the aim of the preceding paragraph, land, sea and air forces, as well as other war potential, will never be maintained. The right of belligerency of the state will not be recognized."

What if every country had an Article 9 in their constitution?

God of War

By Yorifumi Yaguchi

God of war, sometimes visible and invisible,
Showed up after his work of Terrorism,
Stood on the platform with his baton.

And started conducting,
Then the US high-tech vultures rushed to Afghan
And started unsparing bombardment.

His seeds bore splendid fruit again!
Joy danced on his face.
This god, who has been worshipped

In the mosques
Under the mask of Allah
And in the church

Under the mask of Christ,
has been ceaselessly whispering to them
"Make wars."

From *The Poetry of Yorifumi Yaguchi: A Japanese Voice in English,* ed.
Wilbur J. Birky, Good Books (2006)

IRAQ: WHERE IS THE EVIL?

July 14, 2006

In August 2003, a few months after the US occupation of Iraq began, I joined several co-workers in a visit to Karbala, Najef, and other areas of Southern Shiite Iraq. Karbala is one of the key spiritual centers of the Muslim world, particularly for Shia people. After a full day of discussions with local human rights workers, we were encouraged to visit the shrine where venerated founders of the Shiite movement are entombed. When we reached the mosque, we saw pilgrims crowding the area in an attitude of great veneration.

Within the courtyard under the oppressively hot sun, men and women gathered in groups to pray and bow before the tombs. We walked around the shrine respectfully and tried not to attract attention to ourselves. Outside was a large area where congregants could buy snacks of kebab, vegetables, and sweets from stalls. The sun was setting as we exited. In the distance we could see a massive traffic jam. Only then did we realize how many of the guests had traveled great distances to pray.

In the relaxed festive atmosphere, we noticed that some of the pilgrims kept watching and smiling at us. After a time one of the curious pilgrims asked in perfect English where we were from. I responded that I was from Chicago but others in our group were from Canada. We began to talk, and as he translated, others joined the conversation which quickly became energized as often happens when long separated friends finally meet. It turned out that this group was from Iran. They wanted to know what we did. In turn, we inquired about life in Iran. Their curiosity was as palpable as ours. The tone between us was anything but hostile. We didn't even have time to get frightened about our security. Our conversations ranged over topics like computers, home life, and faith. One of the Iranians insisted on buying snacks for us in a sign of warm hospitality.

When we finally went our separate ways, my heart was pounding. We, children of the Great Satan, had just had an enormously relaxing conversation with citizens whose nation had recently been called a member of the Axis of Evil by the US President. And the conversation occurred in a Holy Place! The meeting at the Karbala shrine probably will have little implication for the resolution of matters relating to who is more evil in the world or who has weapons of mass destruction, but that one moment of companionship reminded me again that humans would do well to exercise some humility in the identification of evil.

Gene and Shia women in Najef, Iraq (2003)

When Presidents or Ayatollahs brashly name a place "evil," we get very close to the primal sin of the Bible where humans thought that by nibbling the delicious fruits of the tree of the knowledge of good and evil they would gain absolute truth. We human beings really prefer to function as Adam, Eve, and the serpent—each of whom shared complicity in deceiving one another regarding the knowledge of good and evil. The unifying notion is that the tree of life, in its original portrayal, represents a wholeness of the things that make for peace. It does not say that there is no evil, brokenness, or unfinished business; it just suggests that on this question we do well to rein in the blistering overconfidence that locates the source of evil outside ourselves. The original sin is to say that evil resides in another person, organization, ideology, religion, or nation.

When nations or peace groups become too confident about the precise location of evil, their message has a way of becoming lifeless. The sacredness in people and nations is awakened by a vision of wholeness, and a preoccupation with evil at the expense of the good distorts that goal.

There was sacredness to our meeting in the Karbala Holy Place that fatwas (proclamations that carry authority) from Presidents and Ayatollahs are unable to touch in their attempts to divide up the world. The tree of life reminds us of the balance inherent in our work. Too many confident pronouncements on the nature of evil can drag us down. This does not mean we just sit silently and admire the tree of life. No! Enjoy the garden. But recognize the boundaries of knowledge and vision. The Holy is both beyond and within us, something that we can appreciate and enjoy right in our own garden. It is here where the undisturbed creation with its magnificent fruit can inspire us to know our perfect place.

AFGHANISTAN: THE RIGHT TO LIFE

September 2, 2009

On an August day in 2009, in the heart of Kandahar, Afghanistan (population 450,000) a bomb went off killing 43 people. "Anything can happen to ordinary Afghans. We are not safe. We are without value. We have no right to life," said one victim whose family is among the living wounded.

In 2002 I was in Afghanistan with Christian Peacemaker Teams. It was a time of change. Our peacemaking mission was welcomed. People allowed themselves to dream that the 20 years of war that began when the Soviets invaded might be ending. I returned home hoping we could place peacemakers there because I saw signs that unarmed violence reduction could augment what villages, groups, and individuals were already doing.

I listened to village elders describe how they deal with violence, murder, and injustice. I heard them describe the bombs that fell near or on their homes after 9/11. I was surprised by people's candor, their hospitality, and their confident formulas for conflict resolution. I am old enough to know that hospitality may be a means of masking the truth, but I also know that by accepting their generosity we each became more persuaded of one another's sincerity.

I saw rubble and rusting hulks from the Soviet period and acres of destroyed city where warlords once fought for spoils. On the road to Bagram Air Force Base I witnessed deserted fields, irrigation systems, and villages where crops of wheat and vegetables once fed people of Kabul. "Where have you been all these years?" asked an Afghan when he heard we were from the group working for peace. Similar sentiments were voiced in small gestures of kindness and big dreams shared privately over tea.

I learned from seasoned Afghans that armed and uniformed soldiers would have great difficulty creating the conditions for reconciliation. I wanted to be honest but I worried that the Taliban and the war lords would ignore my fumbling peace probes. Being a foreigner, particularly an American, didn't help. After decades of work in conflict situations I had learned to live with my uncertainty. My instinct told me to test various words, actions, and suggestions in conditions where violent conflict resolution had become routine. Surprise! Something usually works even when society seems to be coming apart.

The signs of the futility of foreign military intervention have been evident for at least eight years, and for centuries, for those who take the time to read the pointers in Afghan history. When a nation is submerged in the political economy of war, turning the dial in a new direction is difficult to do. The promise of more foreign troops erects a higher threshold. Neither drones, F 15s, nor brilliantly trained marines can find the path to a new political economy where the things that make for peace sprout and blossom. If promises of crop improvement and new infrastructure are clothed in combat, all chances for real security are lost.

Suspicion and opportunism always win in conditions of war. We should not be surprised by the daily rants from the foreign press describing corruption and opportunism. War and development don't mix. Even the recent elections are exercises in political entertainment, devoid of trust. The prevailing socio-cultural mindset that violence can be redemptive simply does not work.

As American or Canadian or British soldiers continue to depart for the conflicted front, I hope someone tells them about the kindness of the Afghan people and advises them to listen in ways that generations before them could not. If they do listen they may come home early, not because of bullet wounds, but because they learned that they were sent into a conundrum of the impossible. They will remember the wise voices in the villages. For some foreign soldiers those voices will resonate because their hearts have been prepared. For them this will launch a new vision that includes all of humanity. I want to support them.

The US and its NATO partners are tired. The people of Kandahar are tired. Everyone is less secure. The 2500 Canadian soldiers in Kandahar, like their partners to the south, are stuck. The Canadian people and their military anxiously await 2011 when the government has promised to end the military "mission." Meantime the US is preparing to deploy 20,000 additional soldiers. Without a "right to life" where is the hope? The way we invest in Afghanistan is more costly and treacherous than security swaps on Wall Street. Must we wait until all sides are exhausted before we end the reliance on military solutions?

THE AFGHAN WAR IS BAD FOR MY HEALTH

July 18, 2009

For the past eight years I have been thinking about what we can do for Afghans who ask, "Where have you been"? People of Peace, let us find our voices. Here are four suggestions.

1. Listening delegations can be organized to spend time in Afghanistan to learn and to feel the void of meaning in the violence. Their experience will rev up all of us to engage in peacemaking.

2. Local communities who listen to returning soldiers can help them sort out their perceptions and feelings and it will help us complete at least a piece of our own story. What have the soldiers learned from the Afghan people? What have they learned about war? About this war? About themselves? About what is worth living for and dying for?

3. At town hall meetings or in phone calls to legislators how about a simple message, "The Afghan War is bad for my health."

4. Find the local and national organizations who are already working on these items.

For people of faith there must be a response to the plaintive words from Kandahar, "We have no right to life." When I came back from Afghanistan in 2002, despite my best efforts I could not find the people and financial support to place teams there. A whole team of peacemakers could have been placed for the cost of just one foreign soldier. And for the cost of another soldier several local teams could have been trained and put to work. Those bold words are still calling out to me. "Where have you been all these years?" And, where are we now?

I still can't figure out where hope comes from. I don't have a formula. But, I do know that for me, hope had to rise from the ashes of disappointment in my country and disappointment about all the man-made sacred movements. Hope for me came to rest on the confidence that Spirit works in its time. And, thankfully the Spirit doesn't put all the weight on my shoulders alone.

- From Darkness Before Dawn

PEACEMAKING AND BADAL

(REVENGE)

June 24, 2009

Viewed from the stance of many Pukhtoon villagers the wars in Afghanistan and Pakistan, stretching back to the arrival of Soviet forces in Afghanistan in the early '80s, have already lasted almost 30 years. According to Ali Gohar, a respected leader in the Pukhtoon communities of Northwest Pakistan and Afghanistan, any peace negotiations must be conditioned by customary law. He summarizes this in a recent monograph, "Hospitality is one of the finest virtues, revenge a sacred duty, and bravery an essential pre-requisite for an honorable life."

If the perpetrator of an offense has not made authentic amends, Badal (revenge) is the duty of a Pukhtoon. Those who invade and those who bomb with drones or airplanes are seen as guilty of crimes. The obligation of Badal rests with the aggrieved party and it can be discharged only by action against the aggressor, writes Gohar. If there is no means of revenge it may be deferred for years, but it is disgraceful to abandon it entirely.

I asked persons who live in the midst of Pukhtoon tribal society if there is any way that these tribal customs can become a resource for peace rather than a source of conflict. Their answer was an unqualified "Yes." "But," said one person with deep roots in the region, "you cannot send people from the military—you must send civilians. We will not trust the military who send Hellfire missiles, bombs, and soldiers."

When I asked my hosts if it would be safe for someone to come and talk, they replied, "We honor our guests with our lives. They will be welcomed by a row of local people who shoot their weapons into the air as a sign of hospitality. We will guard you with our lives."

BACHA KHAN: PAKISTAN'S NONVIOLENT WARRIOR

November 11, 2007

"I am going to give you such a weapon that the police and the army will not be able to stand against it. It is the weapon of the Prophet, but you are not aware of it. That weapon is patience and righteousness. No power on earth can stand against it." —Abdul Ghaffar Khan, Muslim leader of the Pukhtoon nonviolent army that worked against British rule in the 1920s.

In late 2001 and early 2002 I had occasion to meet with people in the northwest frontier city of Peshawar, Pakistan, and surrounding areas where millions of Pukhtoon Afghans still live. I have always said that if I had ten lives, one of them would be in India as an Indian. In early 2002 I added Pakistan to the list of nations for one of my ten lives. My engagement with Pakistani secular society and unfolding Muslim culture grew deeper every day, and when I departed my personal journey with people building on the work of Bacha Khan had only begun.

For thousands of years Pakistan's dense mountainous western border with Afghanistan where Pukhtoon people live has escaped the grip of empires.

Today the rebellious and independent threads running through those mountains have been temporarily renamed "Al Qaeda supporters" or "Taliban protectors." More than two millennia ago Alexander the Great reached the edge of the Indus Valley by leading his army through these mountains before heading back home. In ancient times some of our common ancestors, the Aryan peoples from Central Asia, also reached Pakistan's Indus Valley and the land of India beyond. Since Alexander the Great, foreign forces from the west and east have met successive defeats in Afghanistan often at the hands of the Pukhtoon people.

As early converts to Islam, the Pukhtoon tribes embraced and integrated Islam into their ancient cultural framework of tough independence. When their way of life was threatened by the Soviets, their fighters welcomed the generous outpouring of US support channeled largely through Pakistan's military during the 1980s.

Until this century, these areas were loosely administered by political officers in a system begun by the British (though the British never really controlled the area) and continued in the period of independent Pakistan. Until Pakistan was enlisted as a major player in the war on Soviet intervention in Afghanistan those policies were continued by Pakistan. Now the US Special Forces, building on the often failed experience of the last 25 years, plan to work with the Pakistani military to bring the area under discipline and end the terrorist threat.

A major legacy for Pakistan, of the US-supported defeat of the Soviet Union in Afghanistan, has been growth in modern military competence and an increase in militant Islam. Specialized schools called Madrasas, selected military and intelligence units, Pakistani military personnel and civilians find meaning for their lives in more activist pursuits.

British and Soviet invasions of Afghanistan were turned back by the crafty tactics of the Pukhtoon people. Eventually the British and their Soviet successors gave up. Given US injection of even wider military support to Pakistan, it would seem that few lessons have been learned. Today the generals in Pakistan know that trying to quell Pukhtoon dissent may be an unrealistic goal. But they are willing to carry on counterinsurgency in a perfunctory way to keep generous US military aid flowing. The Pakistani military sees itself as the single unifying institution in the nation, the only body able to balance the secular and constitutional peoples of Pakistan's heartland with the nation's Islamic vision.

Pakistan has a civil society built on the living memory of the nonviolent struggle leading to the independence of India and Pakistan 60 years ago. Bacha Khan, quoted at the beginning of this article, was a Pukhtoon leader of one part of that effort. A committed Muslim, he worked with Gandhi in the struggle against British rule. Khan founded the Khudai Khidmatgar (Servants of God) known as the Red Shirts. They formed around the notion of Satyagraha, active nonviolence. One hundred thousand participants were recruited into one of history's largest nonviolent armies. The Red Shirt soldiers became legendary for dying at the hands of the British police and military.

When I visited Peshawar in 2001, I found interest in the nonviolent struggle of 85 years ago again weaving its way through Pakistan's world. Little reported because of the world's fascination with terrorism and entertainment violence, the legacy of Bacha Khan survives although the man and his nonviolent army have been long forgotten. This legacy is a restraining influence on unbridled military rule, and gives legitimacy to the group of lawyers who now man the barricades and advocate the rule of law.

In Peshawar I visited a private organization that provided educational programs to remote villages in Afghanistan during the long night of Taliban rule. My colleague, Doug Pritchard and I drank tea and waited for the agency's director in the entry hall. Finally our host arrived. His first words to us were, "Peacemaker Teams, where have you been all these years?" We felt those words coming from the deepest chambers of his heart. He described his work and his vision. He also described the enormous levels of violence experienced by his people. He recalled his childhood in Pukhtoon villages where blood feuds led to killing long after the initial incident or insult. He invited us to think together about peacemaking strategies and about building a broad culture of peace.

Now as the violence in Afghanistan increases and the military gains even more prominence in Pakistan I remember my Pukhtoon friends in Peshawar and Kabul. I remember their invitation for us to work with them. I remember their urgent words. And I remember our inability to respond then with teams of trained and committed people. The absence of sustained support for grass roots peacemaking is one part of a puzzle that led to conditions for emergency military rule and new US initiatives to send Special Forces. Oh Lord how long?

RETOOLED MYTHS FROM VIETNAM AND IRAQ

March 31, 2008

While history never repeats itself there are myth-like patterns that are recycled. We rely upon myths to explain war, peace, politics, and the heavens. As part of our collective story, myths become more visible in times of war.

With mandarin statues at the tomb of Emperor Khai Dinh, outside Hue, Vietnam (2009)

The following five myths about US involvement in Iraq were already alive during the Vietnam War 40 years ago.

MYTH I: Blame the Victim

Turn on your TV and you will hear politicians announce another ringing critique of the Iraqi government for failing to bring all Iraqis together in unity to fight terror. The Iraqis are regularly chastised for dithering over how the vast oil resources will be apportioned. And as they did during the Vietnam War, opportunistic politicians and trickster columnists charge Iraqis, often correctly, with reckless disregard for human rights. The lack of progress is the fault of the Iraqis. If they just did what we think should be done everything could be fixed.

For ten years during the Vietnam War we heard a steady cacophony of voices from liberals, conservatives, and even critics of the war claiming that the South Vietnamese government, which was propped up by the US, was not democratic and repressed its people. Blaming language was used by war proponents and critics. A long term strategy that emphasized negotiations and humanity instead of war-making might have moved the world community in positive ways.

MYTH II: If We Believe We Are Helping It Must Be OK

In the early years of the Iraq war I spent many days seeking out military officials of the occupation. As I waited with Iraqi family victims to solicit information about detainees, often with little result, I talked with young officers and soldiers about the US mission. In those days when US hope for success had not yet yielded to disenchantment I was often told, "We are just here to help the Iraqis help themselves and then we will go home."

My mind flashed back to Vietnam where I first encountered these innocent statements of purpose, often combined with talk of "hearts and minds." In Vietnam I thought this was a newly minted rallying cry just for that war. Forty years later I realize that these sincere lines about helping have been woven through wars against aboriginal peoples, the Philippine war, and other imperialist adventures. I cringed when I heard those words in Iraq. My Iraqi co-workers listened politely to the soldiers, as did the Vietnamese many years ago, but they grasped the patronizing implications of this deeply held myth.

Myths like "We are just here to help the people" are deeply imbedded within us. That is why preachers, generals, politicians, candidates, and sincere soldiers use these words with such powerful effect.

MYTH III: War Helps Human Rights

As I made my rounds to military offices in Baghdad I never found an officer or soldier who spoke disparagingly about human rights. In fact for some, the elimination of Saddam and the Baathist party rule was one of the greatest contributions to humanity in this age. Some at mid and lower levels were genuinely frustrated that more could not be done for Iraqis who had disappeared in the detention system. One sergeant hugged me as I left his squad. He told me that I was doing important work and hinted that he would like to join the group that I was with. Soldiers with so much good will were still unable to protect prisoners at Abu Ghraib.

Nor did the soldiers' good will protect us from ethnic cleansing, suicide bombers, independent armies, and other forms of terror that swallowed up the tidy conversations about human rights in the years that followed. In Iraq the humanitarian rules of warfare have taken a step backward. The use of terror on both sides characterized the conflict in Vietnam too, where both sides appealed to the temporary use of violence in the form of bombs and assassination programs, all, it was claimed, in the interest of a greater good.

MYTH IV: Our Exit Will Bring Greater Violence

When I finish my speeches a predictable question is, "Don't we have to stay now because if we leave things will get worse? Won't our departure lead to balkanization, greater instability and a larger blood bath?' The language is almost identical to what I heard 40 years ago during the Vietnam War. The myth says that US forces, aid, and advice must continue in order to make things less violent and more democratic.

The presence of foreign military players distorts the behaviors of people and institutions who, under local mores and for religious or nationalist reasons, would not necessarily seek redress with guns or suicide killings. That presence, in effect, puts off the day when the diverse components of society can evolve in their own way by negotiations and confrontation towards greater participation and democracy. No military power or outside mediator can make things come out right. In their own time local processes will allow a new balance. The unified Vietnam 33 years after the war ended, though imperfect in its respect for diversity, may in fact help everyone see long term hope for Iraq if foreign troops and US policies get out of the way.

MYTH V: These People Have Always Been at War
History is often written to emphasize epic wars. But the myth, that the history of other societies is a continuous litany of war, is false. The sub text of this myth is that, unlike us, "those" people are wired for killing and war at a deep level. I invite you to travel the world with me to visit the families of victims wherever they survive and you will be disabused. If we train ourselves to listen we will find deeply rooted threads of peacemaking in every tradition.

As children of an enlightened age we have become conscious of the power of these myths. Humans use stories about enemies to justify killing the enemy. Over time these narratives root themselves deep in our psyche. When we live off the power of these beliefs we weaken ourselves and make the world more dangerous. It takes energy, hard work, and conscious effort not to become victims of the damage that myths unleash in our minds.

Those of us who live by the convictions of love for friend and foe alike are also invited to remind ourselves that this love is only convincing when it is grounded in real life and actions. Ours is a living story and yet one that is far from complete. Words strike the opening chord, but the symphony is completed with action. Our vision of the peaceable world can become truncated and used as a club for manipulation by preachers, generals, and politicians and sometimes even by ourselves. I wish I could tell you that the world could be neatly separated between those who embrace only the good myths and those who embrace only the bad. But it is not so. The myths of epic battles, violence, and separation have life in all of us and it takes generations to infuse ourselves with the habits of love.

PART III

THE PRACTICE OF
PEACEMAKING

For most of his life Gene immersed himself in peace action or focused on building the scaffolding that would allow others to engage. He rarely wrote about what he did, though he examined political and economic trends to aid in recognizing the signs of the times. His personal and orga-nizational approach helped to create space for unexpected outcomes. He also recognized that peacemakers face obstacles, many of them internal, and if acknowledged, can be addressed in order to release energy for life-giving action. This section is finally the vintage Gene reflecting on his work.

Section A

CREATE SPACE FOR UNEXPECTED OUTCOMES

CREATING SPACE

August 1, 2007

In the early 1990s I joined a group of six people in Miami, Florida, where Haitian boat people, refugees from the Haitian military regime, were being held by US officials in detention facilities. Many had fled life threatening circumstances in Haiti only to be detained by the US Coast Guard when their overloaded ships arrived on US shores. The federal authorities denied our group entrance to the detention facility to speak with the Haitian refugees. Our goal was to give greater visibility to the refugees so that a just and humane solution could be reached.

Finally after two days of quiet vigils and of building rapport with officials, we decided to push the envelope a little further. We purchased several bottles of bubbles usually designed for children's play. The next day at our vigil we alerted

> Gene had a way of cutting to the soul of things. All of us who knew him will have had the experience of coming away startled and sometimes a little unnerved by his incisive challenges to our assumptions concerning issues under discussion. Our perceptions of the world were changed by our encounters with him.
>
> - *Harold Neufeld*, Winnipeg, Manitoba.

supporters and the press that we would be blowing bubbles into the prison facilities with sacred messages of freedom for Haitian boat people. When we arrived to carry out our action the guards took up their normal positions. We prayed, sang one song, and began blowing bubbles towards the prison facility. Fortunately a slight breeze carried some of our bubbles all the way to the prison facilities. Of course, the guards became curious and wanted to know immediately what the bubble blowing was about.

We explained that since we were prohibited from entering we decided to blow these bubbles towards the facility. We explained further that these were not just normal bubbles, that they had power and were carrying special messages for the release of Haitians held inside. We warned the guards that since these were blessed it would be better for them not to try to touch the bubbles but rather to allow them to reach their intended destination. The guards cooperated and their behavior suggested that we had found a thoughtful way to carry our message. To others who came and went, we explained the meaning of the bubbles through leaflets and conversations.

This light-hearted, yet serious, action helped to create something we might call *space for unexpected outcomes*. Word of the bubbles spread. Unknown to us, another delegation was also at the prison attempting to interview Haitian detainees for a national organization of human rights lawyers. The group contacted us immediately when they saw the bubbles and even joined in the vigil although they may not have been familiar with our style. They had received permission to visit the prison but none of them spoke Creole. One of our group was fluent and that person was immediately certified to join the lawyers on the following day for interviews. Our two groups agreed to coordinate our work. The innocence of children's bubbles lowered the level of threat on all sides and created space for several days of interviews and vigils. Both kinds of work were needed in the long struggle to provide a pathway towards normalization in Haiti and to bring about greater safety for refugees. No one would consider the action a final answer. However it did bring about a context for change.

Gene paved the way for many of us to deepen our journeys and relationships. I remember his laugh, his contemplations, and his ability to create space and possibility.

- *Kristin Anderson-Rosetti, Ravenna, Italy*

Creating space in peacemaking means fashioning a place in time where sights, sounds, feelings, words, or art are presented within the context of a nonviolent perspective. This space can have both external and internal dimensions. The external space reaches across rigid boundaries set by governments and security institutions. The internal space in the actors on all sides invites a spirit of flexibility and openness. When space for openness happens in a non-judgmental spirit, the hardened lines of thinking are freer to reach for new possibilities. Something new can be born.

This newness requires the confidence to innovate and an abandonment of rigid and ritualized positions. In the absence of this safe zone, a new reality is not possible, and positions harden. So for example, the judgments of Chiefs of States like Saddam Hussein and George Bush prevented each of them from considering options other than intransigence and war. Inflexible thinking insists that honor and respect for the nation can be sustained only by guns, killing, and bombs.

Creative space is not the product of weakness, capitulation, or fear. It does not arise out of hardness, stubbornness, or cramped thinking. Because this place combines external and internal dimensions it can be sensed through body language, as well as words, or expressions of hospitality. Creative space is recognized as safe for all participants.

> I will always cherish the memories – the laughter, the booming voice. Gene sitting in the living room with the colorful Iraqi hat. I remember him ringing the bell from the Chicago temple with us following, towards the Federal Plaza in a mock funeral march, protesting and mourning the loss of both Americans and Iraqis to the Desert Storm war. The voice of a Man of Peace has gone quiet but there will be many others.
>
> - *Edna Montemayor,*
> *Chicago, Illinois*

People who are in jail always have the option of sustaining the flexibility and freedom of their internal space. History documents the treasured stories of perseverance and even joy in well known personalities like Nelson Mandela and others who endured jail in their struggles for religious freedoms.

Could such a space have been created before the outbreak of the Iraq war where all participants might have recognized the logic of a less violent way? Conflicts are rarely solved at the level at which they are created. Solutions require a shift of mindset which can be brought about, traditionally, by elders or other wise members of the community or, in modern parlance, facilitators and peacemakers.

The new place that we are looking for invites access to all the possibilities of the five senses. In some cases a clearly articulated, holistic position can move things along. In other cases, surprise or artistic expression can set the stage for the universal imagination to manifest itself. And sometimes a deliberate statement of moral sensitivity and rootedness in faith can awaken interest because of its reference to transcendence.

When peacemaker teams joined with Colombians to find a way for refugee villagers to return to their land, the imbalance between four different armed groups on the one hand and the refugees and peacemaker teams on the other was weighted in favor of the people with guns. By preaching or yelling at or leafleting any of the armed groups we would have accomplished little and may have increased the danger for everyone. However, the sight of one or two unarmed peacemaker canoes on the Opon River, the only means of travel to and from the villages, helped keep armed groups at a distance. Some of the assassinations continued further up river and the violence was not completely stopped. Gas continued to be stolen from nearby government pipelines by armed actors. But a context for new thinking was created. The refugees returned.

Before the war broke out in Iraq, our peacemaker team tried to imagine how an action like a boat trip down the Tigrés River loaded with olive oil might help send the world and the two contending nations the necessary energy and firm resolve to awaken the interior lights of George Bush and Saddam Hussein. A similar boat on the Mississippi River loaded with canola oil may have extended the rippling space for life in the other country. But the problem was not only in George Bush or Saddam Hussein; the problem resided in us too. We failed to find a mode or symbol for creation. We may have been too lacking in imagination, too fearful of failure and of looking dumb. We may have come too late to the place of conflict so that, without the experience and credibility, we lacked the authority to kindle the imagination of Iraqis and of peacemakers from the outside.

The public ministries of great teachers often begin with marginalized populations, in villages and market towns. When Jesus entered a village, he often joined an event where new thinking about God and human beings became possible. He used a healing, a marriage celebration, or even an upside down imitation of politicians as in his entry into Jerusalem on a peasant's donkey. These well timed events were easily understood by ordinary people. Some responded enthusiastically and others were outraged. The space that opened up shook the ground and rearranged long held convictions, even to the point of challenging whole systems. Some people were inclined to dig in. But for many, it was a space that pointed to the sacred knowing that leads to peace.

MY TRAVELING COMPANIONS AS I GO TO WASHINGTON, DC

December 24, 2005

Tomorrow I depart from my hideaway in Northwestern Ontario for Washington DC resuming my citizenship in the nation in which I was born. On Sunday we will begin 14 days of processions to Shine the Light on the shadowy and public sources of war (the World Bank-IMF, State Department, Pentagon) that have contributed to our contemporary culture of violence. Am I confident that we will make any difference? No! Am I confident that this is the right thing to do? Yes.

It's been 38 years since I did my first public witness on the question of war and it was clear to me then in Saigon, that actions speak louder than words. Nevertheless, I have never started or joined these kinds of events without the ghosts of nagging doubt pecking away at me in the back of my head. Maybe I just don't pray enough.

Here are the names of a few of those ghosts. Mr. Ghost Leave Things Alone tells me that we might make things worse because there are sensitive things that governments have to do and I don't know all the facts. Mr. Ghost Arrogance reminds me that using the language *Shine the Light* is arrogant, possibly moralistic, and points a finger of guilt at someone else in such a way that I come off as holier than thou. Mr. Bad Manners Ghost hisses that I am just one more eccentric, misguided and irrelevant, maybe fanatical do gooder. When will I learn to be nicer? Mr. Image Ghost keeps me awake at night blabbering that unless I have wide and positive media coverage I will have failed. Well thank you Mr. Image Ghost, I have been around long enough to know that the work of peace will not be done in a single public event. And Mr. Media Ghost, I know you are looking for a good story and might even be open to some suggestions. And then there is the Ghost of Authority, who nibbles away at my confidence. By what authority do you speak of these things? What gives you the confidence to take this on, to take on all shadowy wars? Good questions. I can give you my bio which will help but probably won't satisfy your bothersome questions.

These voices are my companions as I travel to Washington, where I will hold my flashlight or torch, trying to shine a little light. I know these voices well. They show up every time. Occasionally they are successful and win their arguments. When they all cooperate and speak at once they can drive me to silence, not the good kind of silence that opens me to the light of God, but the bad kind that makes me depressed.

Even though I have witnessed the power of light to overcome dangerous shadowy stuff for 38 years, these little guys still take up a lot of my time.

So what do I want to ask of you, my friends? I know a call for prayer can be transforming and it can also be a cop out. We have tried to listen to God in our preparations but I know that even those phrases can be infected with dishonesty. So I leave your support in your hands. If you have the gift of prayer and know it down deep, pray that the Glory of God would be revealed. That is a very big prayer, big enough to cover all of us and our ghosts.

WHY I LIKE SANTA CLAUS

December 22, 2009

Santa Claus was never a big part of my life until I let my white beard grow long. That was twenty years ago. My beard sometimes closes doors to North American Caucasians who think I never got out of the 1960s but the beard opens many portals to wonderful conversations in places like Vietnam, where they called me Karl Marx. Elders in Afghanistan admired it and apparently trusted me more because of it. They addressed me as Baba (Uncle) Noel. Once at the Mexico City airport I got stopped eleven times by mothers with young children who wanted their child to meet Señor Noel. It was summer and I didn't have a single gift to give, not even a piece of hard tack candy.

When late November arrives, I know I am in for surprise greetings every time I go out. The words from strangers carry positive energy. People have good thoughts about Santa, with the exception of children aged seven and older who have become suspicious that Santa talk is a ruse.

The home I grew up in acknowledged Santa. We didn't have a fireplace, so it was confusing to me how Santa would get into the house by way of a chimney that went to a coal furnace. Somehow he made it in, and the stockings were full when I awoke on Christmas day. There was at least one small present, an orange and some hard tack candy. Not my favorite, but I didn't complain because I didn't want to stop a good thing.

I first became aware of the power of Santa and St. Nicholas during the 1990s when I regularly visited Palestine where Muslims, Jews, and Christians alike used my appearance as a conversation starter. When the second intifada (uprising) broke out in 2000, there were violent exchanges between Israelis and Christian villages like Beit Jala, near Bethlehem. In Beit Jala I was seriously introduced to St. Nicholas, their patron saint who gave special protection to the villagers.

The original Saint Nicholas lived in 4th century Turkey in the city of Myra and was known to be a prolific and secret gift giver, particularly to people who left their shoes out for him. According

> I will really miss Gene's blog column —and my white bearded Santa.
> - *Sr. Pilar Verzosa, Religious of the Good Shepherd, Quezon City, Philippines*

to legend, St. Nicholas spoke up for justice and was imprisoned under the Roman emperor, Diocletian. He later became a bishop and participated in the Council of Nicaea after he was released from prison by Emperor Constantine, the first emperor to court the support of Christians. When he died, a unique relic called *manna*, which had special healing powers, formed on his coffin.

The merging of Santa Claus, in his flying sleigh, and St. Nicholas, the gift giver and healer, with the birth of Jesus has really only happened in the last several hundred years. The designation of December 25 to remember Jesus' birth didn't occur until 350 years after Jesus' birth. It is almost certainly not Jesus' birthday. It is winter in Palestine and shepherds are not likely to be in the fields. The date was probably chosen because it was the Roman holiday that celebrated the winter solstice in the Northern hemisphere. Today Christian and non Christian cultures alike celebrate Christmas.

In our time the holiday season has become a marriage of commerce and advent that conveniently invokes Santa to escape the more demanding implications of Jesus' birth in its original context of poverty and the politics of domination, along with the themes of universal peace. The power of Santa is invoked to sell lots of stuff. In fact, the whole economic year hangs on December sales and by the time Santa Claus has worked his wonders in the market place he has been thoroughly trivialized.

I have never played Santa for a commercial establishment, but I have impersonated Santa for events of gift giving. Commercial establishments need a lift from Santa because it is very hard to sell Christmas shoppers on a story about someone being born in a stable with goat manure on the dirt floor.

One time I visited Toys R Us dressed like Santa and accompanied by a team of elves. It was a few days after Christmas so the symbolism was still solidly implanted in people's brains. We entered the store and immediately requested the manager to remove violent war toys from his shelves. I explained to him how dangerous the toys were and that I had determined that the bad toys must be permanently removed for the safety of children. He replied that what was on his shelves was not my business to which I replied that toys are always my business.

We then used the shopping carts to load assorted dangerous toys. By that time the police had decided to intervene in what they called a disturbance but what we designated a "recall." TV cameras were also present. I informed the police that my staff and I would leave the store as soon as we had completed our work. The police threatened arrest. We had a quick staff meeting—elves and Santa—and judged that the police would never arrest Santa. We were right. However, the police blocked our progress as we pushed our carts from aisle to aisle and finally into the backroom where we instructed the workers to hold the toys for pick up by United Postal Service and prompt shipment to my workshop.

So you see Santa can be firm and hardnosed. That is why hardnosed adults should put Santa Claus and his ancient partner Saint Nicholas back into the holiday season!

Gene plays Santa at the Rainy River First Nations seniors' Christmas party (2008).

LETTERS FROM CREECH AIR FORCE BASE

JUMPSTART IMAGINATION

March 28, 2009

In these closing days of Lent, I will be joining a vigil at Creech Air Force Base west of Las Vegas. Yesterday, national news agencies reported stepped up Unmanned Arial Systems (UAS), or drone missile, attacks directed at villages in Western Pakistan and Eastern Afghanistan. The attacks are now reaching further South and increasing in number.

We are gathering to vigil at Creech because the UAS air missiles are controlled from there by specially trained pilots and navigators who huddle in front of vast rooms of monitors and send digital signals of instruction that drop bombs and collect information as the drones hover over villages.

The attacks are not just killing people; they are making enemies in a time when people need to be talking to each other in the sectors where attacks are happening. They spread suspicion in the Pakistani and Afghan communities. "Who is telling the Americans to do this?" they ask.

Drones like the MQ 1 Predator are the most recent instrument in the long search for a cleaner, safer battlefield where attacking an enemy involves less risk. Crossbows, poison gas, aero planes, nuclear weapons, Agent Orange, smart bombs, and other vehicles litter the history of this search for the perfect weapon. Promising less risk for "our" soldiers, these digital weapons are popular with politicians.

By joining this vigil at the place where these weapons are commanded I hope to deepen my own consciousness about the state of violence in the world. I also hope to jump start my own imagination in three areas. How do I understand and communicate the danger, risk, and ethical implications of digital warfare? How do I awaken my own sensitivity to villagers' travail of danger and death in Afghanistan and Pakistan? How do I integrate all of this to the central theme of Lent, overcoming violence through sacrifice and new life?

GROUND THE DRONES

April 7, 2009

It is 7:06 in the morning. The first *MQ 9 Reaper Hunter/Killer* drone is just taking off. This practice take-off and landing maneuver will follow every 18 minutes throughout the morning. I have joined the group this Holy Week to vigil and pray under the banner *Ground the Drones*. Training for the deployment and control of these aircraft for their mission of information gathering and destruction in Afghanistan and Pakistan is headquartered here at Creech Air Force Base in Nevada, 40 miles northwest of Las Vegas. A major upgrade of the first predator which was armed with two missiles and is still widely used, the reaper is capable of carrying 14 Hellfire missiles.

Our group has enjoyed an almost cordial welcome from base workers, pilots, officers, and enlisted personnel. Many of them occasionally toot their horns, wave, or flash the V sign as they enter and depart the base. Between these signs of positive connection are challenges. A man rolled down his window yesterday and shouted at me, "Do you have any idea how many American soldiers' lives are saved every day by these aircraft?" I replied that I didn't know and he advised me that the true number of saved service lives was 20 to 30 per day. I have not been able to confirm these numbers from any scientific source but I did remind him that the drone aircraft create enormous hostility in Afghanistan, Pakistan, and Iraq that will take generations to overcome. He was not impressed.

Flight crews of two, including a pilot and a technician called a sensor sit in front of computer monitors and digitally guide these craft as they perform their long-distance missions. The pilot is experienced, but the sensor is fresh from basic training and technical school. A chaplain from the base told a colleague at our vigil that disturbing dysfunctions are beginning to show up among people who control these aircraft.

These drones are capable of remaining airborne for extended periods. According to the International Online Defense Magazine, "The availability of high performance sensors and large capacity of precision guided weapons enable the new Predator to operate as an efficient 'Hunter Killer' platform, seeking and engaging targets at high probability of success." The Reaper, also known as Predator II, began flying missions in 2007. It was pressed into service, according to Defense Magazine, because it filled a gap "between conflicting demands for payload, altitude, speed and persistence." Unlike the first generation Predator, the Reaper can fly at an altitude of 50,000 feet.

In the coming years the full implications of the transformation of the US military to digital warfare will become apparent. The outrage we see in the countries where drones are used and the signs of trauma already becoming visible among soldiers, designers, and victims will signal a new era of brokenness. Yesterday US Secretary of Defense Gates announced a 127% increase in funding for drones and other digitally guided military hardware. These crafts are much cheaper and believed to be less risky for military personnel than more expensive weapons like the $350 million dollar F 122 whose production is to be cancelled.

Our local communities in the US host the corporations that develop these new and smarter instruments of war. The workers who build them, the designers who create them and the operators of these wily crafts, worship in our churches. The Indian Springs Motor Motel where our vigil group has rented a room for logistical support is packed solid with young marines, here for some last minute training in desert warfare and basic training in the new age of digital warfare. They are friendly and serious, and some are worried. Yesterday morning two of them described their ambivalence as they recovered from a hard night on the town. In a few days they will be off to the front lines.

About three hundred yards from the main entrance to Creech is a small building set aside for two-week training programs for military chaplains who are about to depart for Afghanistan and Iraq. We know that the military chaplain is one of the first to be contacted by soldiers who are disturbed and morally shaken by what they experience in combat. Every month dozens seek a way out and often encounter enormous difficulty and little support even from chaplains, all of whom come from religious traditions that teach love.

Like the chaplains, all of us who claim faith are invited to reach deep into the wealth of our traditions and discern what our responses can be. We will be further enabled to do this when our religious support structures—churches and denominational institutions—also reach deep into the peaceful and humanizing resources of holy tradition. The desert here in Indian Springs, Nevada, where native people once came for water to sustain life, is waiting for the transformation inherent in faith and in the traditions that uphold life.

ENTER THE BASE, SINGING

April 14, 2009

On Thursday, April 9, the day before Good Friday, participants in the vigil to Ground the Drones entered Creech Air Force Base in Indian Springs, Nevada, with the goal of meeting with commanders and pilots. The 14 people from all over the US crossed onto the base just before rush hour singing, "When the Saints Go Marching In."

By extending the 10-day vigil of prayer and Holy Communication from the base entrance more directly to the people inside, we underlined the urgent need to think about the implications of unmanned Predators dropping their deadly bombs on civilians in Afghanistan or Pakistan. All the vigil participants who entered the base were arrested. The vigil and the entry into Creech AFB are a public cry to think about the implications of drone warfare.

Following the entry, confusion reigned as Military Police and contracted guards shuffled about furiously to prevent the group from moving deeper into the base. Some members of the Military Police who had recently returned from Iraq stood with their M16s pointed at those who had entered, who by now were kneeling in prayer just inside the steel gate which had slammed shut behind them.

The sign at the entrance of Creech AFB tells it all: Home of the United States Air Force Desert Warfare Training Center. Pilots, officers, enlisted

people and civilians had passed us all week, many in shiny foreign-built vehicles and some in buses. We waved and prayed for their safety, especially for the Marines who had come for specialized training in desert warfare before deployment. As I stood there I wanted to write a new poster to hold, *Drop the Drones: Develop the People* or *Drones Belong in Bee Hives* but I couldn't find a thick black pen.

Overhead, MQ 9 Reaper Hunter/Killer drones circled every six minutes touching down and taking off again in simulated precision bombing. They also rehearsed techniques for camera use and intelligence gathering. In a few weeks, still from Creech AFB, these pilots and their staffs will be directing craft like these as they take off from Bagram Air Force Base north of Kabul, Afghanistan. Those Predators will deliver Hellfire Missiles and collect information on Pakistan and Afghanistan. I wonder if their powerful cameras took pictures of me as I stood with my sign and, if they did, were the photos printed out and displayed for entertainment over coffee?

Vigil participants remained on their knees on the hard paved road with guns pointed at them until Nevada State Police arrived to write citations. Before their arrest, a military policeman from the air force was ordered to read a statement formally warning the peace warriors, who had been deep in prayer for over an hour, that they would be arrested if they did not leave immediately. I watched with others outside the main entrance to Creech as my colleagues were hauled away in Nevada State Police vehicles.

Eventually all 14 participants were transported to the Las Vegas City jail for a cold overnight stay in a cell where rich and poor, disorderly drunks, addicts, street people, prostitutes, and vagrants are stowed away. According to those arrested there were no criminal Wall Streeters or Bank executives in the Las Vegas jail. My friends were released the next morning, and their final gathering was blessed with a rousing Easter poem urging Jesus to come on out of the tomb!

The Larger Vision: Getting in the Way of War Itself

We are closer than we were 20 years ago when the vision was articulated but we have only made a start, with teams, training, full time workers, reservists, and projects in explosive situations. When we are 20 times as big we can think about standing in front of armies instead of individual soldiers as we do now.

LUCKY IN VEGAS

October 6, 2009

The question of how to respond to America's current wars, its plans for dominance in space, and to the unfolding movement of robotic warfare challenges all of us to think in fresh ways. The collapse of worldwide finance, with the accompanying loss of confidence in the big players, may also be creating a greater space for imagination. I am done with letting the big players and gaming machines control the culture. Whatever else it may be, economics is also a matter of spirit. Truth happens in experiments, and is backed by courage and preparedness for the teachable moment. My time in Las Vegas was one such moment.

Near the end of my time there, I participated at a consultation among peace activists in the desert sands not far from the Creech Air Force Base where pilots are trained for robotic warfare. At one point I complained to Vincent Harding, one of the other participants, that I still had little confidence in deciding what to do, and he gave me a little pastoral advice from an African proverb. "How do you eat an elephant?" he asked. The answer: "One bite at a time."

A new window on the bullying power of finance capital would open for me a little later, in the biggest detention center of Las Vegas. But first I had to go to the base, where I wanted to meet a commander to discuss Predator I and II, the drones I had heard so much about from Pakistani people when I visited them in June. I joined a group of seven and we began to walk along the commercial entrance to Creech AFB. We were soon detained behind a large concrete barricade by the Clark County police. As we were transferred to the care of military police who pointed their big black guns at us, I thought about the finances that pay for Creech.

While we waited in front of the guns to be transported to Clark County Detention Center, two blocks from the Golden Nugget casino, someone asked me to kill time, for the benefit of my fellow detainees and our guards, with a full voiced report on my recent trip to Pakistan. I could not serve tea, as my Pakistani friends would have, but I was able to represent truthfully what I had learned about their fears of becoming the targets of Predator drones, and about their hopes for an unfolding of peace in South Asia.

By midnight, six hours after the pilgrimage into Creech had begun, I had been fingerprinted several times, questioned repeatedly, tested for TB and had my blood pressure checked. I was asked if I had recently tried to commit suicide, and I repeatedly spelled my last name for the vast Las Vegas criminal bureaucracy I was relieved of my shoes, socks, watch, ID, money—everything but my pants and shirt. Later in the night I was pushed into a 10 by 20 foot holding cell where 18 others were already making some kind of peace or silently plotting revenge at police who had insulted them on their road to detention.

The sounds within the cell included broad snores, other bodily noises, and loud television—a cacophony that reminded us we had reached a peculiar moment of truth. By approximately 4 a.m. a gruel-like slop arrived for breakfast. Nausea teased our stomach muscles. The guards had thoughtfully placed a large plastic bag in the middle of the floor and told us to put any leftovers in it. "If you make a 'blankety blank' mess," the guard screamed, "you can plan to be in the holding area for two more weeks." By the time of my release the second and third "grueling" meals had come and gone. As the hours passed, I got to know my cell mates. Several had been picked up for jay walking (evidently a matter of major concern in Las Vegas), others for traffic violations. Everyone except me had some other kind of out-standing legal problem. For several men, it was a simple matter of records never having been updated.

My loss of shoes and socks became a matter of considerable concern since the temperature in the holding area is just south of a cool fall day near the south polar ice cap. While the street people slept through the fog, as though it were just another day on the tracks, the rest of us shared our stories.

One high roller was being tracked for outstanding debts of $125,000 at two casinos when he was stopped on a traffic violation. A few phone calls later he zipped up his $700 shoes and was off to another race. He told me he had once won $600,000 in two hours, but he admitted his career on the strip had cost his family a lot more than he had won. When I told the group that I was in for "disturbing the war" at Creech AFB I got modest applause, enough to wake up some of the dedicated sleepers.

Actually, I think I got lucky in Vegas because I was introduced to at least two angels-in-waiting. I haven't had a chance, yet, to talk to them very much. You see, angels always come to me in upsetting ways. First, the angel of unearned and unconscious powerlessness showed up at the gathering of peace activists. I will be talking to that angel. The second appeared both in the shouts of the Clark County Sheriff's officers and in the close-up and personal discussions with other detained people. My cell mates were curious about Afghanistan and Pakistan, but they also reminded me to watch out for bully behavior wherever it shows up—in Afghanistan, in police uniforms, on the back streets of Vegas or on Wall Street. I will be having more conversations with this angel. The light and dark of the desert has gotten me revved up again.

Gene Stoltzfus' Spirit Present at Trial

By Peter Ediger, Pace e Bene Las Vegas, Nevada, September 21, 2010

While not present in the flesh, the spirit of Gene Stoltzfus was in evidence at the recent trial of the "Creech 14" in Las Vegas, Nevada. Gene was a supporter of those arrested on April 9, 2009, after entering the Creech Air Force base at Indian Springs in an attempt to hand deliver a letter to the base commander. The letter expressed concerns about the use of drones for surveillance and combat to hunt down and kill people in Afghanistan, Pakistan and other lands. Gene carried a personal interest in this issue, having visited Pakistan earlier in 2009, hearing stories from people related to victims of drone attacks. Gene had planned to come back to Nevada for another week of witness at Creech in April of this 2010, but he died several weeks earlier.

The 14 activists had their day in Clark County Court on Tuesday, September 21. After stating at the opening that the defense could only discuss matters related to the charge of misdemeanor trespass, Judge William Jansen nevertheless allowed each of the three expert witnesses to testify at length, weaving together the justification of necessity making it not only a right but sometimes a duty to engage in trespass, with the Nuremburg principles and issues of international law as it relates to targeted killing.

After a moving closing statement by defendants, Judge Jansen, obviously affected by the testimony, stated that given the important issues raised, he would need several months to study the matter before he would give a written decision. The defendants and supporters applauded when Judge Jansen left the courtroom saying, "Go in peace." My eyes flowed tears of joy. I felt the spirit of Gene Stoltzfus hovering.

In the celebration which followed this inspiring morning, the community of witnesses and supporters included a time for sharing memories of Gene. Judy Homanich, one of the Creech 14, had prepared beautiful bookmarks with a photo of Gene.

Gene's farewell blessing at retreat, August 2004

STUDY TRENDS, INFLUENCE POLICIES

RESPONSIBILITY TO PROTECT: HOW DO WE DO IT?

May 28, 2008

The "Responsibility to Protect" (R2P) doctrine gives international support to a new standard for intervention to protect civilians when a state cannot or will not protect its people. The standard calls for an armed and trained United Nations (UN) peacekeeping force of thousands, but emphasizes humanitarian intervention as well. This plan, which grew out of the Millennium Goals set by the UN in 2001, would place soldiers under international command in nasty situations like Rwanda, Darfur, Burma, Zimbabwe, and Palestine. It would also respond to civic and police violence in cities, and perhaps in places where aboriginal people are under attack. R2P is modeled, in part, on fifty years of Canada's valuable contribution to peace-keeping using armed soldiers, a practice now largely abandoned.

In a time when worldwide initiatives in peacemaker teams and conflict resolution enjoy exceptional success, this proposal concerns us because it relies again on the possibility of military intervention. Filipino sociology professor and Congressman, Walden Bello, a scholar with a comprehensive grasp of globalization, suggests that the doctrine of Responsibility to Protect adopted by the UN Security Council Resolution 1674 on April 28, 2006 may simply be a sanitized version of modern imperialism. He contends that the doctrine challenges the centuries-old covenant that respects the sovereignty of states. However, in order for there to be a practical and credible critique of armed intervention, the efforts of non-violent conflict resolution practitioners and peacemakers must be multiplied many times over.

At the root of this discussion is our understanding that a basic shift is necessary in our assumptions about how violence is overcome. The idea that violence can be held in check and perhaps melted by non-violent means is good news to a lot of people. It is bad news for those who are stuck in old ways. While the growth and success of conflict resolution initiatives should not surprise us, it often does. Perhaps this is because in our darker moments all of us are tempted to submit to the deeply held myths surrounding the effectiveness of armed intervention. Our habit of armed intervention as a means of resolution reaches back to the very beginnings of organized warfare in the land of Iraq 5000 years ago. In fact, the military has become the premier symbol of nationhood and empire. Nations and empires turn to their soldiers because there is nothing else available that they think will work. So the military is invoked to address the issues. Nations generally think in the short term and they resist change. Breaking the habits of armed soldiering in the way we organize the world will require generations of effort and experimentation.

People of many religious faiths agree that they have a responsibility to protect and assist vulnerable victims and the R2P doctrine has received ecumenical church support. Christian support for the proposal builds, in part, on millennium-long reflection and negotiation with the New Testament themes of enemy loving that culminated in the compromise doctrine of just war which, since the 4th century, has been widely and variously applied. Ecclesiastical support for this doctrine implies that the deployment of armed soldiers to bring about greater justice, human rights, and political order by force is a legitimate enterprise. This is at least one significant step removed from direct involvement, personal risk, or immediate engagement by churches.

Some years ago I visited our Christian Peacemaker Team (CPT) in Colombia. The day before my arrival the team received an emergency call from a remote village where armed conflict had broken out between groups allied to the government and underground forces. The people urgently requested a presence of protection and I traveled to the village with Scott Kerr, an experienced CPT member. By the time we reached the village, more than half the people had fled and the fire fight was over. Those who remained were terrorized because they knew that both sides of the belligerent forces would return and charge individuals in the community with collaboration which could lead to capture or execution.

Two hours after we arrived an armed group of thirty entered the village and began going house to house while their commander sat down to visit. My experienced partner talked to him softly and firmly, requesting that his soldiers not enter houses. He explained that visiting these homes would make the occupants targets of his enemy. Within minutes the commander had ordered soldiers not to enter houses, and within an hour his unit moved out. Later in the day representatives from a rival group arrived and were similarly encouraged to respect the locals. I believe our presence may have saved lives and property, and affected the future of the community.

This story illustrates how an unarmed presence can be effective where an armed presence may have been less effective. The unarmed presence creates space for people to make decisions about their own lives, whereas an armed presence imposes compliance and may awaken fear. My hunch is that unarmed peacemakers are also less at risk.

Christians around the world, with the exception of some groups in the US, met the threat of war in Iraq with a greater unity of opposition than we have seen in many centuries of war. This opposition emanated from a variety of sources. It resulted, in part, from serious engagement with the Bible, and from a worldwide renaissance of interest in the Gospel of Peace. Some was the product of personal experience with war and violence in the last century. Some of the motivation came from local political culture. This renewed interest represents an enormous opportunity to deepen our faith in the Good News of Peace and to organize ourselves to turn back violence in places where people are vulnerable. This is not the time to negotiate away pacifism and the many ongoing experiments to develop methods of non-violent intervention.

> I'd been waiting for this. Big important questions that only Gene could answer.
> **"Would you shoot?"** asked I. Would you shoot, gun in pocket, and thugs with machetes on mother and child right in front of you? Thinking to myself: I likely would. A thoughtful response which took a lifetime to develop. I'm hanging on every word, listening carefully. Something about getting in the way, doing work ahead of time, putting your life on the line – about how one violent act will cause another and then another. What else did he say now?
> I won't shoot next time.
>
> - *Shaun Loney, Founding Director of BUILD, Winnipeg, Manitoba*

But in our enthusiasm a thread of humility is vital. While an armed international peacekeeping force is not a satisfying solution, outright rejection of this option may not be a complete answer either. None of us has invented the perfect path to overcoming violence with love. All of us who strive to create official or private initiatives of violence reduction cooperate, at some point, with armed groups like the paramilitary or the police—occasionally with some success, but more often with disappointing results. I have yet to meet an armed group that doesn't at some point abuse its power, or become destructive in the pursuit of "just" goals.

Often, when presenting these convictions, the first question I am asked is, "What if Hitler had not been stopped?" My response: "When Jesus said, 'blessed are the peacemakers' he offered us a vision of how things might be different. That difference requires moral fortitude, training and the willingness to assume risk. What if Christians had taken the generic New Testament teachings of peacemaking literally and refused to join Hitler's armies? What if Christians had refused to participate in the plantation system before the American civil war?"

Transformation comes out of the mysterious meeting or clash, sometimes heated, between individuals or groups. For transformation to be the means to new reality, only one side of the engagement need be in touch with the infinite power of charity, love or agape whichever word you like. Usually some of that resource is embedded within both parties because it has been given to all of us, although we find so many ways to forget or avoid it.

February 7, 2008

What future do we foresee if we cannot do better? Can our world overcome its superstitious embrace of arms without the gentle but persistent reminders of people who use only the strength of words, body language, and organized truth telling? If Christians can't figure out a way, we may have to admit that an armed interventionist strategy is the answer and we may have to get behind it with money, people, and organization.

But *what if*? What if Christians and others could break away from the addiction to the force of arms and find ways to get things to come out right? What if, in this century, we determine to build on the successful experiments in non-violent enemy loving which are arising even out of the horrible conflicts of the last century?

MERCENARY WARFARE

March 3, 2010

In April 2004 the world awoke to a horrible scene in Fallujah, Iraq. Insurgents had ambushed a vehicle carrying civilian US government mercenary contractors and killed them. Two of the burned corpses were hung from a bridge in downtown Fallujah where they dangled for several days as photos of them flashed around the world. Commentators immediately compared the Fallujah footage to that of dead American soldiers dragged through the streets of Mogadishu, Somalia in 1993. The victims in Somalia were American soldiers. The victims in Fallujah were American mercenaries employed by Blackwater Inc, renamed XE in 2007.

In this century we are entering a new era of mercenary warriors. From the strategic point of view, modern mercenaries fulfill a crucial requirement. They provide logistical and selected security support for invading forces in the field. In addition, at the political level they allow policy makers to engage in off-the-record, arms length, and clandestine activities on the margins of—and outside of—the law. This allows what is formally called "plausible deniability." In the recent past mercenary soldiers for hire have also served in

Bosnia, Liberia, Pakistan, and Rwanda. They have guarded Afghan President Karzai and built detention facilities in Guantanamo and elsewhere. On February 10, 2010, the Iraqi government ordered Blackwater Inc. and all of its subsidiaries to leave Iraq or risk arrest. The order included Blackwater employees involved in the deadly shooting incident in 2007 which killed 17 civilians in Baghdad's Nisour Square.

Due to a hostile local population, the occupation of Iraq and the war in Afghanistan have required heavily armed guards, escorts, and sharpshooters to provide logistical protection for the millions of tons of military supplies. It is dangerous work and requires people who have been trained. The contractors, some from Third World nations like the Philippines, also staff the kitchens, the PXs, tax-free general stores for soldiers, and provide thousands of other support activities. Most mercenary contractors who carry out security related functions are former military personnel. The Pentagon argues that, despite lavish salaries, using military contractors is cheaper than training soldiers for the work. What is not said is that if the American armed forces were to carry out all these tasks the US Government would have to implement an unpopular military draft and expose the sons and perhaps the daughters of the privileged classes to the dangers and inconveniences of military service.

Paramilitary units in Colombia, Philippines, Haiti, Afghanistan, and many other countries around the world perform functions similar to those performed by private sector mercenaries for US forces in Iraq and Afghanistan. US operatives, sometimes together with mercenaries, have been involved in strategy formation, training, and sometimes financing, usually in conjunction with local government military groups. Even the Taliban got its start in the early 1980s as a paramilitary project developed and financed by US personnel in conjunction with the governments of Pakistan and Saudi Arabia. Like the mercenary soldiers of Blackwater, virtually all of whom have had careers in the US military, the Taliban grew up fighting and, to this day, this is the only profession they really know.

The Taliban and Colombian thug-like paramilitary units function at the margins of their traditional customary law. Modern mercenary contractors often also function outside our constitutional law.

Both blur the lines between judicial process and police activity, arrogating to themselves life and death decisions that, in any responsible society, must be legislated. These soldiers know the law of the gun. When or if constitutional government is restored they seek a place within the institutions of security work, but rarely abandon their habits of threatening, killing, and improvising seat-of-the-pants law enforcement. Former Secretary of Defense Donald Rumsfeld insisted that war using mercenary contractors is cheaper but his calculations failed to include the costs of re-educating the first generation of Taliban fighters and assimilating them back into civilian life after combat with the Soviets in the 1980s. Nor did his calculations include the cost to the American people of the expansion of its imperial culture of security.

Mercenaries working under private corporations have also carried out specialized tasks for the CIA including the loading of Hellfire missiles onto Predator drones. They have engaged in search, capture or assassination of enemy leaders in areas like the borderlands of Afghanistan and Pakistan. Officially, the Blackwater mercenaries killed in Fallujah in 2004 were in the line of duty "to protect food shipments." However, doubt exists as to whether or not there were, in fact, any food shipments that day.

In 2003-4 I made several trips to Iraq. At the close of the first trip, an Iraqi with whom I had consulted extensively rushed to the Christian Peace-maker Teams (CPT) apartment. He insisted that I meet with some very important people for an extended lunch just sixteen hours before I was to

Members of Voices for Creative Non-Violence in Pakistan (2009)

depart from Baghdad. Our CPT schedule was piled full of planning and projects. I didn't want to go because I suspected I was about to be the recipient of a mountainous request that CPT had neither the personnel nor the money to respond to. But I agreed to go with other CPTers. About two-thirds of the way through the introductions I figured it out; the dinner was a gathering of leaders from some of the senior families of Fallujah. I waited, knowing that they wanted something.

They asked about CPT. I knew that they already knew a great deal because two persons in the circle had spent extended time with us. We explained our decision to focus on detainees, house raids, and the rights of Iraqis. We gave two examples of cases we were working on. We were frank about our limitations. There was some silence. Then one person asked if we ever did anything outside of Baghdad, and whether we had ever been in Fallujah. I thought I knew where the conversation was going so I asked no more questions, hoping that the conversation about Fallujah would not develop. I didn't want them to ask if we could put a team in Fallujah. They persisted with broad hints about the needs of Fallujah.

As I left that meeting, the spokesperson of the group took me aside. He identified himself as a senior police officer in Iraq. As he prepared to speak to me his cell phone rang. It was his counterpart, a US colonel. I waited and tried not to listen to what was being said. The call ended. He looked at me and said, "The US Forces detained my nephew some weeks ago. We can't find him. Could CPT help us find my nephew?" I said we could try although our team was already over committed. We did try but we were not successful. I don't know if his nephew survived detention. I don't know if the police officer survived the last seven years.

This encounter took place six months before the first battle of Fallujah

I'd been waiting for this. Big important questions that only Gene could answer.

"Do you have regrets?" asked my young voice. Because I do. I always do.

The horror in Fallujah, Iraq. "I came home on schedule," he said. "I feel like if we had gone there we could have stopped all that misery," he said. Speaking like an army general, he talked about pouring peacemakers in. "If only I'd stayed. We could have stopped them."

He believed he could stop the US Army. And I believed him.

- Shaun Loney, Founding Director of BUILD, Winnipeg, Manitoba

which followed the killing of the Blackwater contractors. As I write this I wonder how many of the people in that circle on that day are still alive in Iraq or have any normalcy in their lives. I wonder if an unarmed peacemaking team in Fallujah might have made a real difference to the US strategy that led not once but twice to the destruction of that city. I believe trained and disciplined unarmed peacemakers in sufficient numbers could have done, without arms, what armed soldiers could not accomplish; namely, protect the people of Fallujah.

The story does not have to end here. We are not condemned to surviving in a world where the law is decimated by successive generations of paramilitaries. But the answer will probably not come from the Pentagon nor from the White House which may not be able to escape the grasp of a citizenry whose houses of worship celebrate the institutions of violent intervention. Congressional efforts to rein in support for paramilitaries or mercenaries have been timid. We will know if unarmed spiritually based peacemakers can do this when we become even more resolved to create a corps that can be present in the Fallujahs that are still waiting to happen.

Every one of us is impacted by a dominant culture that insists that police or military force will make things right. Every day this culture tells us that dirty tricks, usually done in secret, are required for our survival and that someone (why not Blackwater?) has to do this dirty, but noble work. It will take an expanding worldwide, grass roots culture reaching beyond national borders to fashion a body of Christian peacemakers who can be an effective power to block the guns and be part of transforming each impending tragedy of war. Little by little there will be change.

ROBOTIC WARFARE: MAKING THIS WORLD SAFE?

February 25, 2010

The protection of civilians has been a fundamental principle in the defense of the just war doctrine for more than 1600 years. The increase in the killing of civilians, by both national and insurgent forces, and the corollary use of civilians as human shields often go unnoticed. The use of robotic warfare may push this tendency even further, and it broadly reflects a trend that, in modern times, stretches from fire bombings in Dresden and atomic destruction in Hiroshima to the use of IEDs in Iraq and drones in Pakistan

Last week Predator drones attacked Helmand province in Southern Afghanistan and killed an unknown number of civilians. Incidents such as this reinforce the messages of protest that Pakistanis have been trying to send Americans for the past few years. Despite the much ballyhooed 'precision' of these aircrafts and their weapons, they still kill civilians because corroborating intelligence on the ground is unreliable, leading to flawed targeting.

During the final week of Lent I expect to travel again to the Creech Air Force Base just outside Las Vegas, the training and operations headquarters for Predator drone systems. From here remote pilots and their staff guide the planes in 24-hour surveillance and attack assignments over Pakistan, Iraq and Afghanistan. I go knowing that the Predators are just the visible tip of a vast array of robotic technology now being developed to make modern warfare "safer" for soldiers but, inevitably, more lethal for civilians.

Predators and their Hellfire missiles are the system of choice just now, but maybe not for long. Like conventional aircraft, large Predators have a lot of problems. Although cheaper than earlier generations of bombers, they are still expensive to build, maintain, and fly. They can also be easy to spot. In Pakistan I was told that children in remote areas have a game they call "spotting the Predators." Shrinking those vehicles to just a few ounces will change more than children's games on the ground; it will permit a much closer view of who's doing what, where, and when.

Clearly, work of disarmament will be complicated by the deployment of small robotic instruments of all kinds. The US Army is working with universities to build tiny, bird-like "microfliers" to be used by its Micro Autonomous Systems and Technology Collaborative Alliance for intelligence gathering and surveillance. Joseph Mait, manager of the Army Research Laboratory says, "Our long-term goal is to develop technologies that can produce a map of a building interior or detect bombs."

> At one time it may have been possible to be a wedge into the organized violent suppression of violence by simply refusing military service. For most of us that expression of pacifism, refusal to join the military, is no longer the only critical boundary for a life of peacemaking.

According to Discovery Magazine, Haibo Dong of Wright State University is working on a four-winged robot, the Wright Dragon flyer. The designers complain that it is more difficult to create than a two-winged flapping system but that it promises more speed and maneuverability. Dong expects to have a prototype, about the size of a real dragon-fly, completed this year. "This small craft could perform surveillance, environmental monitoring, and search and rescue," he says.

At Harvard University roboticist Robert Wood is working on mechanical bee-like instruments to create a colony of RoboBees. These swarming robots will incorporate optical and chemical sensors as well as communications systems to make autonomous flight decisions and to coordinate with colony members during tasks such as searching for objects or people.

Robotic technology is already heavily used in all of America's wars with as many as 4000 robots on the ground in Iraq. Tiny information gathering devices are complemented by robotic instruments designed to identify and disarm bombs. With ground mobility they can enter into dangerous settings where enemy soldiers are heavily armed. Some of these instruments are being adapted for, or are already being used for homeland security. Their phenomenal growth will forever change police work, the arms race, and the balance of power in the world.

What are the ethical implications of this revolution of arms, force, and information gathering?

A robotic arms race is underway with development, deployment, and use of robotic warfare already taking place in at least 40 countries around the world. There are few if any forums that address the implications of this race for the future of life on earth and for the quality of life issues such as basic freedoms.

As the robotic arms movement unfolds, the possibilities for backyard development of instruments of destruction exceed the limits of imagination. Violent video games were just a beginning and they may be helping to dull

our sensitivity. The IED (improvised explosive device), an interim defense and attack instrument for insurgents, will have been just the first generation of a long line of sophisticated adaptations of off the shelf technology for killing. The distance between the safe researcher silently working in a sanitized laboratory and the field practitioner is narrowing. The absence of meaningful work for so many in this generation may become the void where new waves of imagination in the service of violence are unleashed. Non-violence movements will match this challenge only with solid healthy organizations and a keen understanding of the implications of robotic developments.

As civilian casualties grow, persons who believe that life is sacred are faced with enormous new challenges. Peacemakers and human rights workers have only begun to grasp the implications of robotic warfare. People on the ground in Pakistan told me that just 10% of the victims of Predator drone bombings are insurgent combatants; 90% are civilians. The Pakistan Security Monitor, a project of the School for International Studies at Simon Fraser University disputes these figures. I have travelled in Pakistan and have heard the 90% estimate from persons with access to the areas of impact, along with accompanying stories of travail and death to women and children.

On this frontier of ethics and robotic warfare, our methods of witness for a non-violent way will be forced to adapt. The reach of research, development, and manufacture dips into every one of our communities. The development and manufacture of killer instruments is no longer limited to a small number of corporations. We are swimming in a culture of robotics and we can watch in admiration or distaste as the magic is unveiled. Today ordinary people can go to their local computer store or to *amazon.com* to order component parts for assembling a weapon. What will we do when the com-

As I study digitally networked warfare, I notice that there are very few people thinking about the global consequences of this new mode of warfare. I can understand why any military body would want to find the perfect weapon – a weapon that ensures victory, kills fewer people (particularly one's own), does less collateral damage, and maybe makes fewer people mad. When gun powder was invented and perfected, those who owned it thought they had such a weapon. It didn't work out, of course, because over several centuries everyone had gun powder. Today's accelerated pace of invention means that the innovations of centuries are telescoped into just a few weeks.

One of my favourite activist stories of Gene involved the time he went with a group of young people to one of those new electronic video game trade fairs where they try out new games on the public. Games for young people have become increasingly violent in the past few decades. They decided to play every game as pacifists, choosing the least violent option available in the video drama. This way of playing was of course counter to the intent of the game-makers and skewed rather considerably the interactive stats they were trying to collect over the day. After a few hours they were found out by the managers of the fair and booted from the premises. Gene told us this story with great humour several years later, his eyes twinkling mischievously.

- Di Brandt, Canada Research Chair in Literature and Creative Writing, Brandon University, Brandon, Manitoba

puter store owner turns out to be a member of our church, synagogue, or temple? What will we do when people in our place of worship own stock in companies that produce the components? In this period of transition and unfolding violence, it may take a little time for our consciences to be awakened. Hopefully our stubborn resistance can be expressed clearly without our falling into legalism. And when we are prepared, we won't have to go to Washington or to some well-mannered legislative office to begin the discussion and to engage in public witness. We start in our local community.

NAVIGATE THE OBSTACLES

TELL US WHAT TO DO!

December 22, 2005

What can we do when the damp numbness of discouragement or despair threatens to shut us down? Without presuming to tell you what to do, let me share what I have learned during my experience with CPT in those times when silence comes upon us and we feel ourselves—individually and collectively—withdrawing into that place where doubt forms, where we lose confidence in our ability to respond to situations, and where our trust in each other is tested.

Here is what sometimes happened to me when I tried to reclaim that place within where belief in enemy loving, nonviolent love, sacrifice and reconciliation once transformed me to embody a vision of something worth living for. My sadness and confusion gave rise to guilt that I had started something that I could not finish. Or, I questioned if I'd been wrong to develop programs in such exposed conditions. In the hour of testing, the vision in which I had placed so much confidence seemed to grow faint. Was this just another romantic dream?

I am ashamed to admit how often I have been through this valley of the shadow of death, even though I know it can happen to any Christian peace person. It's just the way it is. In a romance novel everything turns out well. But in life the good is not a destination; the good is the journey itself, and the choices we make moment to moment. Most importantly, it is not simply a personal walk; it is a communal journey. So let's reflect together on this journey of Christian peacemaking.

During the years I was with CPT, our teams tried to begin the day with common worship. I am sure our primitive attempts at worship must have looked wimpy to our Muslim friends whose ritual of five prayer periods every day was so clear and confident. When life got more dangerous and severe, Muslims' prayer time became more disciplined. I began to notice that our worship too—our songs, scripture readings, and prayers—became more focused at times when we felt threatened, demeaned, or desperate to break through the silence with acts of love.

Now let me get to my point. Elite education or money is not the prerequisite to begin prayerful peace action. The most important elements are prayer, discipline, continuity within the group, and a broad diversity of talents and perspectives. Begin the journey here.

Right now, we need 1000 peacemaker groups in Christian congregations and parishes. Go to your pastor or priest, or to your Christian education director and say, "I want to invite a group of four to eight people to join me in weekly peacemaker prayer and action." If Sunday school hour is too short, plan your events for an evening or for a Saturday morning. Tell your congregation what you are doing and keep them posted. Don't hide what you are doing even if you suspect that it might lead to conflict. This is God's work.

Expect disagreement and expect unity. Expect surprise. Try to fashion your group so that it includes young and old, male and female. Cultural diversity also helps a lot. Now you are on the way. You have taken a big step to a safer, terror-free world for your children's children. There is going to be a lot to do. There will be voices of caution and times when everything you want to do can't be done in one meeting time a week. What you do is going to come right out of your own imagination awakened by the Spirit within you. You will be renewed on your journey.

ACTIVISTS: HOW TO THRIVE IN RECESSION

January 13, 2010

Grassroots organizations are feeling the impact of the recession and are anxious about their futures. All of us, including our natural partners overseas—peace and environmental groups, community organizations—know

At the Mennonite Church Conference information booth (1998). Gene highlights CPT Campaign for Secure Dwellings in Hebron District.

that there is no magic formula that will guarantee the survival of a small grassroots organization. Large foundations will continue to fund large, established organizations, and governments will always favor groups that are mainstream and generally uncritical. In an economic system that reserves the lion's share of profits for those at the top, Wall Street executives and traders will get bonuses this year worth $25 billion, while the vast majority—individuals and organizations alike—including those living at subsistence levels, are taking cuts.

Some grassroots organizations will not recover. When they do not, let us honor the good work they have done and celebrate the emergence of the fresh initiatives that will take their place. Those organizations that survive likely enjoy exceptional leadership and a diverse, committed membership and support community that doesn't resort to blaming and backbiting in times of hardship.

Four Tips for Thriving In Difficult Times

1. *A diverse funding base that relies on individuals, community groups, and religious bodies is always better than relying on a single source.*

   I was once a member of an organization that received almost all its support from a single government source. It had done excellent work in grass roots international development, even speaking out against US Government policies during the Vietnam War. At board meeting after board meeting, we wrung our hands in search of grass roots fundraising models. In the 1990s even the limited government support faded and the organization closed. Nothing worked well enough and the organization had to terminate projects. If early on we had worked for a more diversified and community-based support, we could have continued some very innovative work.

2. *During recovery, reach out and enlarge your support circle, rather than hunkering down and adopting a mindset of scarcity and retreat.*

   I worked briefly with one organization that had to cut expenditures during an income drop. The ensuing process exposed a long-hidden set of grievances including sexism, racism, and religious favoritism. The workplace atmosphere became so intolerable that it's hard to imagine how organizational consultants could have been helpful. The experience reminded me how much work we have to do to enlarge our circles of trust long before the fury of financial crisis explodes. The threat of lay-offs carries a high psychic cost, both for individual employees and for the organization as a whole. One group I know minimized the pain by accepting a staff-wide pay cut of 10%.

3. *Revisit the vision and its supporters*

Under the pressure of crisis it can be tempting to forget the original vision that brought the group together. Some might advocate creating a new vision, forgetting that, as in the case of Native American warriors, authentic vision questing is usually done by individuals. More likely, this is a time for a re-vision quest, a moment in the life of the organization to clarify that part of the vision which keeps it financially viable. Personal visits with financial supporters may be called for in order to assess levels of ongoing support. If funding sources are limited to just one or two major funders, prospects for survival may be precarious and personal visits are imperative. Financial supporters of an organization want reassurance that the project they are supporting is healthy in three fundamental ways: a) that its people remain committed b) that the program remains clear, well articulated, and coordinated c) that the finances are managed responsibly. Personal contact reminds supporters that their ideas and hopes and commitments count.

4. *Expect to be surprised*

An enduring feature of our work is the element of surprise. People involved in social justice work know this but sometimes forget that even in the most desperate situations there can be moments when good things happen unexpectedly. The adjustments we face in times of crisis must be grounded in spiritual energy and kindness. The breath of God and the light of the Spirit create surprises. Surprise and joy, steeped in humor, often arrive just when they are needed most. Witness the folks fighting mountaintop removal in the mining areas of West Virginia. Visit Pakistan, where people are overcoming violence in the midst of chaos.

Observe the peace groups in the Nevada desert who stand united against nuclear bombs. In the work for peace and justice the rewards are much bigger than our survival. So we are able to laugh at our mistakes, joyfully celebrate occasional breakthroughs, and enjoy good meals together. That's where the fun begins.

With Wilson Tan, member of CPT Steering Committee, Singapore,
while on speaking tour in UK (2009)

THE GIFT OF STUBBORN PEOPLE

July 6, 2006

Thirty nine years ago when I returned from Vietnam I discovered a peace community ravaged by internal conflict and controlled by stubborn people who insisted that their way was the right way, the only way. Frequently, when I spoke across the country about the need to end the war, I was savagely attacked by people outraged that I failed to condemn the US Government for genocide or present direct evidence of napalmed villages. In some groups, when I refused to champion Ho Chi Minh and the promise of a communist revolution, my historical and sociological approach to the Vietnamese people was condemned as irrelevant. And sometimes, in churches whose pacifism had survived centuries of testing, my critique of the US was met by silence and the dour, withdrawn faces of those who felt that I was being too harsh in my call to end the war.

Our collective memory of that period is replete with images of stubborn voices sometimes accompanied, we may grant in hindsight, by poor listening skills. But a realistic appraisal of the period also reminds us that enormous positive change came about to curtail the otherwise unlimited exercise of military power. We can all relate stories of great leaps forward due to individuals endowed with the natural gifts of persistence and tenacity. We joke about these people, sometimes out of respect, and sometimes with a residual resentment at having been forced to adapt our own ways.

Stubbornness can be a deeply imbedded, lifelong trait. How it is maintained and manifested—negatively, in struggle against the community, or positively, in the achievement of valuable goals—depends upon the character and consciousness of the individual. It also depends on the capacity of the community to embrace the stubbornness and dialogue with it, and sometimes be changed by it.

Anyone willing to take leadership must have an internal sense of confidence, long term goals, and vision. Leadership cannot simply be a matter of tactics or nice words. Inherent in leadership is a quality of stubbornness which can at times be grating and disruptive of the culture of niceness in churches, organizations, and nations. In a dynamic peace ministry, conflict is inherent and at least temporarily disruptive. This strategic discontinuity is upsetting but necessary in order for change to happen. A constant culture of strategic discontinuity, however, wears people out and ultimately destroys community because no one can survive unlimited conflict.

Stubborn people who are healthy are not static. When their tenacity is coming from an authentic center empowered by the spirit of peace and nonviolence, they will understand that even in their acts of perseverance, new possibilities become visible. To be successful leaders they will have to understand the importance of patience and timing, and they will recognize that their own timetable for action may not be widely held. If they are too rigid they risk being isolated and then their whole vision could be trashed.

What about those of us who hate conflict, and who are easily deflected from our own center by "pushy" people? Remember that the spirit that animates us all comes from the same place. Remember, also, that the last thing the world of peacemaking needs is a bland, soupy consensus that gets nothing done. Persistent engagement is essential for peacemaking and it is no surprise that peace organizations often attract stubborn folks, and that sometimes this results in conflict.

We tend to deal with stubborn folks in one of three ways. Sometimes we isolate them or eject them entirely from the group. Perhaps we can see no alternative, but clearly this is a lose-lose scenario. Sometimes we offer them encouragement to start their own group, overlooking the fact that stubborn people are not always initiators. Again we are both losers. The third alternative is to accept the painful and confrontational processes that might draw us all into a deeper understanding of our mutual needs and goals. This is hard work and does not offer any guarantee that the end product will be better. However, let us remember that the inherent spirit of light and God which comes to us from various sources can sustain, encourage, and provide wide margins of patience.

The intense work of reflection and action required to clarify the purposes and direction of a nonviolent community will never be a "nice" process. Our best example is Jesus, who slogged his way with curious companions through the dusty countryside trying to explain his vision of peace and justice through words and actions. When he entered Jerusalem for the last time his companions, arguing about power structures in a new political order, deserted him in his final act of perseverance. And Jesus, recognizing that no amount of stubbornness could get the point across, took the next step—the cross. Far from ending with his death or with the breakup of the community, however, the story opened up a window through which we can discern radically new ways of getting things done.

At the height of the Vietnam War, all my work seemed to make little difference. Of course I was wrong about that, and over the years I was able to sort out goals and time lines that were realistic. It's the feeling of hopelessness that is so hard to deal with. Failure, hopelessness and even guilt over not doing enough all intermingle. And when you have known the darkness, the light of hope is very precious.

- *Darkness before Dawn, June 4, 2007*

PEACEMAKERS AND ANGER

January 2, 2008

*"Anyone can become angry. That is easy. But to be angry with the right person, to the right degree, at the right time, for the right purpose and in the right way, that is not easy – **Aristotle***

Occasionally, even in the work of peacemaking, blasts of raw emotion overwhelm us without warning, raising our heart rate, tensing our muscles, and affecting our entire being. This, in spite of the fact that we know how disastrous it is to try to solve human problems from a position of anger. Raw anger is devoid of creativity.

In my childhood environment anger was considered wrong in most situations, a solitary emotion best suffered in silence. Gradually this view was tempered by the notion that anger should be "talked out." I learned that bottling up my anger choked off energy, exhausted me, and made me suspicious of the world. I could never sustain long periods of sealed up anger. But letting it out in uncontrolled outbursts accomplished little, and I struggled with the hope that I might become more comfortable with anger.

As I grew in the work of peacemaking I noticed that about once a month a person would enter my life who made me mad during a phone call, a visit or an email exchange. The source was not the warmongers or torturers; rather, these were people I thought I should be working with. I learned that my immediate response was usually not my best. At home, despite my best efforts to conceal my outrage, my wife would notice the signs in my speech or my body language. My first reply to her inquiries was denial. Only after an interlude was useful discussion possible.

Eventually I learned to get over it by talking about it and by writing an angry letter to the person (for my eyes only) and then rereading the letter a day later. By giving myself a day I had time to regain some composure. By then my body language had returned to normal and I would find myself alternating between laughter and embarrassment at what I had written just 24 hours earlier.

In Iraq, Palestine, Vietnam and elsewhere I have listened to stories of prisoners after their release or escape from captivity and torture, and I have been repeatedly impressed that about 85% of them present a calm, reflective, and occasionally humorous manner. They tell me that in prison they learned that anger and its first cousin, hatred, did not help, and that hollering or attacking guards only made things worse. Now that they are free they want to get on with living in such a way that no one else will have to suffer. The insights I have gained from these former captives have often reminded me of what I learned from the stories of the martyrs.

The other 15% continue to be very angry, and they lash out during conversations as though their anger has frozen into hatred. I suspect that their

> Peacemaking work can get heavy especially when one always has to be right. Hard nosed politically correct peacemaking is related to its cousin, hard nosed religiously correct spirituality. I have come to see that true spirituality lives in the uncharted territory between the sacred and the profane. Laughing allows me to go into the unknown. Humor shifts my perspective and allows my body and mind to imagine. By sidestepping my fear I enter into that place where the walls designed to protect me either dissolve or cease to inhibit me. Creativity finds its home here, and new possibilities become visible.
>
> *June 25, 2008*

particular experiences, even earlier in life, have driven them to adopt hatred as the only mode of survival. Perhaps most of us, although we have not been tortured, are tempted to an underlying frozen anger.

It has taken me an embarrassingly long time to discover that anger, properly understood, is an ally and can be a gift for transformation. The lack of mellowing can lead to a state of hatred which is not a base for a workable society. Anger turned inward, prohibits joyfulness. Generations of anger turned inward can create a stifling culture. I wish I had learned 40 years ago to assimilate anger more purposefully into my life and work. I might have been better able to help groups move beyond lifeless "political correctness" and to make real connections.

Traveling on a train in UK (2009)

THOUGHTS ON WHOLENESS AND GUILT

March 25, 2007

The best decisions I have made in my 67 years were not prompted by guilt, but by my sense of what might contribute to the completion of a vision of wholeness—for the world and for myself. But this does not mean that the strong ghost of guilt has not occasionally lifted its head to guide me when I could not hear more compelling voices.

I came to consciousness at a time when the revival movement and its appeal to guilt was on the wane. Its standard conversion formula required giving assent to an essentially unbelievable mechanistic understanding of the meaning of Christ's death and resurrection. Accepting that formula would have infused me with the guilt that comes from dishonest consent.

My road to health as a "recovering revivalist" went through the villages of Vietnam during the war, and through the villages touched by Jesus on the way to Jerusalem where he was handed the death penalty for the crime of sedition and rebellion against government.

In the summer of 1963 I interrupted my sojourn as a seminary student to go to Vietnam as a conscientious objector. I joined International Voluntary

Services (IVS), a primarily secular organization engaged in grassroots development and education. I went just at the time when President John F. Kennedy was increasing the number of American military advisors in an effort to turn back communism and stop a political revolution in progress.

My decision was not a response to guilty feelings about poverty in Vietnam or about discomfort with my country's special calling to pick up where the colonial wars had left off. I went to Vietnam at age 23 because I wanted to complete something in my life and I was open to where that process might lead.

Vietnam (1966)

As I responded to the many new inner voices I heard within, I gained the confidence to test all perceptions of sin, salvation, spirituality, violence, nonviolence, democracy, and revolution. And I see now that my decision couldn't have been more right. If I had heeded the voice of guilt I would have completed seminary and entered one of the church ministries, where I might well have lived in that perpetual cycle of confession and imagined forgiveness so familiar to me from the culture of revivalism.

* * * *

When we began the work of the Christian Peacemaker Teams all branches of the church seemed to adopt a wait-and-see attitude. Would this be a rerun of the strident heavy handed side of the peace movement? Would it just complicate matters by parachuting irresponsible people into difficult situations? Would CPT organizers neglect to root the work in faith? Would it imitate that part of church history that illustrated conflict avoidance? Would it be so "churchy" that it would do little good in the real world?

We realized that our primary task was to carry forward the kind of presence that pointed to truth and opened spaces for the surprises of peacemaking. We knew that the struggle to break through the barriers created by violence would require listening, perseverance, critical reflection, and imaginative, symbolic thinking. We needed to build teams and learn to witness to the possibility of a world without arms. And we had to learn to sing and celebrate, to pray together and cheer each other on.

Many in the church community began to read the Bible teachings on peace with fresh eyes. But the growing acceptance of our work was not matched by an avalanche of CPT volunteers. And I was disappointed most of all by the dearth of workers coming from colleges with peace studies programs.

* * * *

When we enter the world of violence we are entering the sphere of the sacred, a world where the struggle is not only about smart bombs, roadside explosive devices, and intelligence gathering on the enemy. We are entering the world where everyone is asking what is worth living for and what is worth dying for —democracy, truth, God?

At critical moments in my life and work, when various voices competed for attention, I came to believe that all forms of wholeness—personal, social, metaphysical—are interconnected. In my work for peace and against injustice in the midst of war with its starvation, rank injustice and broken spirits, hints of wholeness were already present, and the promise of its fullness hovered beyond the horizon.

For a time I thought this wholeness might come from socialism. Sometimes I thought it might be found in a world-wide peace movement. I also hoped that the one true church would bring spiritual and social wholeness. As those visions merged, and energized and illuminated each other I learned more about the limits of living under the force of guilt.

* * * *

Guilt is heavy and narrow, and it usually comes with clumsy prefigured ideas about how things "ought" to be done. I wish I could say the peace movement in general and the faith-based movements in particular are free from "guilting" people into working for social change. When the movement shows up with heavy handed judgmental attitudes, the energy evaporates through the walls. Guilt-motivated social change workers tend not to stay around very long unless they are made the center of attention. The best antidote to ego-based guilt mongering that I can think of is the development and nurturing of free groups of volunteers who act independently and collectively. Healthy folks shy away from rigid sets of rules and procedures that do not leave room for the spirit of transformative love.

Gene's adventures in the struggle for peace and justice were endlessly fascinating to me; facing down tanks in Manila, standing firm with CPT colleagues to defend a Palestinian family's home against angry crowds, and seemingly always on his way to where the headlines were worst.

But I rarely learned about these things first-hand on his visits because Gene, like Dorothy, was so other-focused and eager to ask questions. Then he would listen to the answers with rapt attention, as though they were precious gifts from an oracle, even if only a recommendation for puncture-proof bicycle tires.

- *Thomas Friesen,*
Vancouver, British Columbia

COURAGE

October 23, 2007

On my upcoming speaking tour on the subject of peacemaking I'm sure to hear the statement, "What you have done is worthy, but I do not have that kind of courage." Usually I hear this, not in public discussion, but in personal encounters afterwards, and I often suspect that it's a way for people to deflect a personal invitation to this way of life. But I see it, also, as evidence of an inner dialogue in motion, engaging them, calling them to deeper living on the basis of core commitments.

Courage is not a domain unique to active peacemakers. Whistle blowers in government, industry and social service agencies risk their careers to report ethical indiscretion in the implementation of public policy, and this is so now widely recognized as a social value that in many countries there is legal protection for whistle blowers. While they are honored for acts of courage on the front lines, soldiers make themselves vulnerable to discipline and isolation for courageously pointing out the failures of the military system.

People of courage rarely consider their actions to have been heroic. They speak, instead, of having been prepared— perhaps by earlier teaching or experience —to act in response to situations. "It just happened because it seemed right," said one of my colleagues who walked alone into a nest of angry soldiers and got them to end the blockade of hundreds of cars and buses. Acts like this are of enormous consequence and, guided by a moral compass somewhere deep within us, they spring at unexpected times from unexpected sources.

> Gene has always been the model for me of faith, integrity, resistance and solidarity. He has helped to challenge me to live with integrity, even when working for institutions which always fall short of the ideals which they/and we, proclaim. I loved that he had no tolerance for BS, whether institutional, political or theological, but always had himself firmly rooted in the every day reality of the oppressed.
>
> *- Doug Hostetter, Director,*
> *Mennonite Central Committee*
> *United Nations Office, New York*

Just this week two career peace workers, Fr. Louie Vitale, O.F.M. and Fr. Steve Kelly, S.J. were sentenced to five months in federal prison for nonviolent action in Fort Huachuca, Arizona, a facility where Army training in torture techniques is carried out. The priests' actions, dramatic on the surface, are routine in the work of peacemaking. Buried in the transcript of the trial testimony were the words of another person whose actions can only be defined as courageous. Major General Antonio M. Taguba served in Iraq and was the primary author of the scathing report on torture at Abu Ghraib which led to an international discussion of human rights. Before the trial General Taguba called the soon to be convicted activists to tell them, "History will honor your actions." What gave the general the courage to write his report knowing it would destroy his chances of further advancement and throw doubts on his honor? Was it his Filipino family roots? His religious upbringing and faith?

I am somewhat familiar with the Abu Ghraib story because it unfolded in 2004 while I was working with our peacemaker team in Baghdad. We had decided to focus on stories of house-raid victims and on the systematic disregard for detainees. We discovered these stories through non-heroic, but often very emotional conversations with families of the victims. As we uncovered patterns of detainee abuse we were able to identify trends and record our findings. We took these materials to the interim authorities—American officers, including senior commanders.

I had some hopes that this work would lead to informed discussion, and that it might become possible for people of courage embedded within the US Army to show some of the moral fiber that had long been planted within them. That courage appeared much sooner than I expected. One soldier made available the photographs of torture at Abu Ghraib that went worldwide. Other soldiers spoke out as well. And when General Taguba's report was released the world was instantly immersed in a fresh conversation about human rights which continues until the present. Although our reports may have been the start, we know that our word alone would not have been sufficient.

The book of Ephesians uses military imagery to remind us to nurture the stuff of courage within ourselves. Long before I eased into the work of peacemaking I was curious about the courage of the people of faith I had read about as a child in *The Martyrs Mirror*. "What gave people the courage to face such unspeakable suffering?" I asked myself time and time again. Rushworth M. Kidder confirms some of my hunches about people of courage in his recent book, *Moral Courage*. He identifies five attributes of courageous people: 1) greater confidence in principles than in personalities, 2) high tolerance for ambiguity, 3) acceptance of deferred gratification and simple rewards, 4) independence of thought, and 5) formidable persistence and determination.

This is not a checklist to use in the heat of the moment when making decisions that might change our lives forever. But it does point us in the directions we might take in structuring our families, our educational institutions, community organizations and churches in order to awaken and nurture the qualities required in moments of decision and action.

My purpose here is not to rally us to run impulsively to the next crisis in our world. Rather, courage is the stuff within that becomes available from the Spirit when the table has been prepared. True courage is not the stuff of ego. What is demanded—the words and actions and sacrifices—will be revealed in the moment of testing. It is true that there is no courage without risk. But the exercise of courage also promises new life, new vision, and hope. Truly courageous acts address and lighten the burdens of all humankind.

BEYOND THE ELECTION

November 3, 2008

Why wait for elections to get down to work or to ignite our hope? We are not powerless nor should we cede important matters to elected officials. Both elections and local efforts for change are messy and often imperfect. But real change comes largely from the participation of grassroots people. Closing a local military base or recruiting office, pressuring an irresponsible corporation to stop producing toxic products, or overturning terrorist style interrogation tactics take five to twenty years or more. Such changes transcend election cycles. Abolition of slavery took more than 100 years and in fact there is still work to be done. The US still has to make good on the 40 acres and a mule promised to the former slaves or their descendants. Effective change requires good strategy carried out by a trained team of people who try all kinds of tactics including delegations, discussions, education, and nonviolent direct action.

Gene and Vietnamese youth flash the peace sign (2009) outside tunnels where North Vietnamese villagers had hidden during US wartime bombings

I have a simple rule for myself in the development of tactics that build on a long term strategy. Two questions keep me on track. Will my words or actions give the people on the other side something to think about or even talk about over coffee? And will my actions awaken positive and uplifting emotional responses from the heart? Maybe you could call this the Stoltzfus Rule of Hearts and Minds.

It is a rare local community that does not have at least one expression of the four global threats—environmental disaster, economic breakdown, a food crisis, and militarism. If 20% of our congregations, mosques, and synagogues would determine as a highest priority to form and support action teams, in five years the world would be on the road to recovery. Over ten years we would see larger solutions beginning to form out of a collage of our efforts. There would be fewer corporations and money managers who try to corner destructive control for quick profit, fewer military bases, more protection for the earth, and the pain of hunger could be narrowed. We will know that the Spirit is in this by the fruits of these efforts.

Gene and the creation of Christian Peacemakers Team was a kind of ongoing case study in creating and sustaining a visionary organization with the unique goal of using nonviolent volunteer peacemakers as agents of change in some of the most troubled places in the world.

Gene was never able to be clear about how he accomplished this massive organization building task. Perhaps that's part of the reason he was so successful. He just tried things out until something worked.

Gene was the delightful outlier who managed to take strong stands and strong actions for peace through his life and simultaneously take the lead in creating an organization, yes even an institution, to reflect those convictions.

- George Lehman, Bluffton University, Bluffton, Ohio

LESSONS I'VE LEARNED

August, 2005

I don't believe that history needs to repeat itself unless we fail to see its lessons. As I look back now at that long, seemingly interminable struggle to end the Vietnam War, I recognize what I learned then and what I wish I had learned.

Gene in the Mennonite Voluntary Service t-shirt (1974)

I wish I had thought much more long term and assembled the educational, speaking, and action projects, with an eye for twenty or fifty years down the road.

I learned that I had to take some time off to heal my own trauma of losing friends, witnessing the effects of battle, and be thankful that I had been preserved for a lifetime of this kind of work.

I learned to listen much more carefully to the angry critics who so often ended up being allies when the time for change came in their own journey. It helped just to be kind to each other.

I said far too many nasty things about "liberals" who said good things but in my narrow thinking didn't do much. My caustic comments didn't help one bit.

I believe a power much greater than myself sustained me and kept me alive. I could have died in Vietnam as several of my friends did.

Las Vegas, Nevada (2009)

I wish I had kept far better records of my work and been more self-critical of our peacemaking projects.

To this day, I thank God that I had really good co-workers.

While I think I learned to read the political tea leaves—the danger and intelligence of the CIA, the danger and the destructiveness of the military, the generous use of the language of terror by the very people who carry out terror—I wish I had integrated the learning more consciously.

I learned to have fun in the work, do a little partying, eat well and, unfortunately, put on too much weight.

I am glad I didn't marry the wonderful women I fell in love with along that part of my journey because both Dorothy and I had to have a little more time to grow up before we could connect.

I learned the value of stubbornness and the need for occasional compromise.

I learned that war is deeply rooted in our worldwide culture and sometimes inside me.

I worked the halls of Congress but I wish I had done more because I learned that there are allies hidden in all sorts of unexpected places (Congress,

State, Defense Department, White House, and down the street in the Bible church, at the Mosque over the hill, in the communist cell). Sometimes it's comfortable to see the world in black and white but real peace warriors see the shades, and it's usually the shadowy area that can save lives, including our own, when the shadow is acknowledged.

I learned to frolic and engage in many unexpected places where I couldn't plan for anything.

I learned that the only fruit of many days of work may be the change of a single adjective in a newspaper article or TV report. I learned that before the action verbs do the hard work there are often many adjective changes.

I began the journey as a child in a fairly small religious group where there were some problems of myopic vision. I learned to treasure parts of that vision. I accepted where I came from and became a citizen of the world and Jesus' follower.

The worldwide development of disciplined peacemaker teams who think long term is the one strategy I know that can roll back the violence of war. I don't know of a better place to start than the worldwide Christian community but the light often appears in unexpected places. Yes, this learning already began during the Vietnam War but the conditions were not in place for the infant to appear until years later.

I learned that history doesn't automatically repeat itself, because people can make choices. Those choices make tiny differences which can create the conditions for massive changes.

When I went to Vietnam I was troubled by the notion that perhaps individuals had no power to make change and that maybe there was no God who cared. By the end of the war, those questions had long been forgotten. I was willing to bet everything on using the little bit of power given me to be part of the bricks and mortar of what wanted to be revealed among the people and cultures of our earth.

PART IV

A LIFE WELL LIVED

Gene was on a life journey to understand how to be a person of peace in the midst of wars and he invited everyone to join the peacemaking party if that's what made their hearts sing. Here are some last words from Gene. We include memorial statements by the CPT co-directors, the Mennonite Church USA, and Gene's sister, Sara Ellen Stoltzfus. The impact of his personal and public life are represented in the reflections by his wife, Dorothy, and Pakistani colleague, Ali Gohar. Please see the Addendum for additional reflections from other people around the world whose lives intersected with Gene's.

LIFETIME PEACEMAKER AWARD

Monday, July 7, 2003

Gene accepted The Peace and Justice Support Network of Mennonite Church USA award "In the name of all my co-workers, some of whom live in very dangerous situations, and who have been sustained by the water of this earth, the water that sustains life in all of us."

Forty years ago yesterday, I arrived in Vietnam and I went from the Saigon Airport to the International Voluntary Services headquarters and then by bus to My Tho, a city in the Mekong Delta to study Vietnamese. The first day off from study was a Sunday. And that Sunday morning, I heard helicopters overhead. I walked to the city's athletic field where helicopters were landing and disgorging Vietnamese soldiers, who had been killed and wounded in a battle 25 kilometers to the west.

This was my introduction to war. It was the beginning of a journey that has lasted 40 years—a journey to understand what it means to be a person of peace in the midst of wars.

Now, here we are in 2003, and our nation is trying to complete the conquest of Iraq, a land that was conquered and pillaged 2300 years ago by Alexander the Great, then by Persia, earlier also by Assyria, and then by the Ottoman Empire. We are part of a long history of conquest and pillaging. One hundred years ago this summer, our nation invaded the Philippines, Puerto Rico, and Cuba—not in self-defense but for economic advantage.

The Christian Peacemaker Teams office, which I work out of, is located in a country where it has become legitimate to discuss being an empire. Last year, I attended a peace meeting where the senior ethicist of the Army War College explained that it was better to do empire, like Pax Romana tried to do, than not do it at all, because Pax Romana brought peace to the entire known world then—and the US can do it today too.

This is the ideology of our time. And it's an ideology based on three components.

- Anti-terrorism—in an earlier era, it might have been called anti-Communism.
- Democracy (our kind)
- Free trade, preferably with an option to support our largest corporations.

So this is the ideology and the world we're a part of, the milieu in which we do our work. The CPT program has projects in Iraq, in Colombia, in the West Bank, and in several native communities in North America,

When CPT began fifteen years ago in 1988, after a long and healthy discussion in our churches, I was asked to be a half-time conductor of the process. I decided at that time that I was not going to worry about that part of the church that didn't approve of active peacemaking. And I believed at that time—and I'm glad I did—that 20 percent of our people would be convinced or have some sense that this might be a good idea to try, or could be tapped for some support. That was about right, I think.

I've often recalled for myself and others our journey by car to a protest in the missile fields of North Dakota one very cold, snowy January day many years back. Gene told me that he had been hired by the church to form resistance communities. How out of the ordinary that was. We both were pleased and amazed. Such was the origins of CPT.

- *Fr. Bob Bossie*, *Eighth Day Center for Justice, Chicago, Illinois*

Now the central idea that we eventually assembled was that disciplined and trained teams of people could be put together, could enter into highly charged, critical situations and could make a difference—make a difference in terms of individual lives, in terms of human rights, and, perhaps, even in terms of the larger fundamental world issues of structural violence. We have done all of those things. Not, of course, without ongoing reflection and the necessary growth and improvement of our work.

The last time I talked with Gene, it was by phone and he asked me a good and profound question, "Have you found your voice?" in relation to the speaking I'd been doing about that whole (CPT hostage) experience. It is a question for a lifetime.

Gene had, it seems to me, an unerring inner compass and he helped me to find my own, even just in brief occasional encounters.

- *James Loney, Toronto, Ontario*

Now, I'd like to talk about the 20 percent, the people who want to work from the foundation of active enemy-loving and nonviolence. This perspective has to literally permeate our lives and, certainly if we went around the room we could point at every one of us and say, "You're not living up to it." But we could also go around the room and cheer one another on, invite each other through our own example to take one more step of faith in the power of love.

Let's remember one piece of our common tradition here—the revival tradition. Now the revival tradition had an invitation. And it's true in that invitation people were sometimes cajoled, sometimes shamed, and sometimes guilted into getting right with God.

Now in peace work and in CPT, we don't want anybody who is too burdened with guilt or shame. But we too issue an invitation to people to come to the table, join the peacemaking party if that's what makes their heart sing. We have fun working together and we don't use "shoulds" and "oughts" and "musts" and "have-tos."

It is all a matter of perspective. We can look around and say, "There's only 30 of us here at this Mennonite peace gathering." Or we can say, "There are only 30 here tonight, but in fact there are thousands of Mennonites who are working at this peace agenda." Which is in fact true.

They are in all kinds of places—in kindergartens, schools, colleges and universities, in community activist groups, in congregations—where they sometimes feel lonely. There are pastors who carry the message in their sermons and counseling or try to do their part in organizing. There are people doing liturgies in local actions, joining CPT teams, people working in Washington, people working through the formal structure of the church. There are thousands of us.

Now I want to share a secret. This is really a good time to be a Mennonite. That might be hard for us to accept, we're supposed to be so humble. But I tell you, it's very good to go around the world and say you're a Mennonite—it really works, it helps. There might come a time when it doesn't help, we don't know. But right now, it works!

So, maybe we were put here for just such a time as this. And if that is the case—and I happen to believe it is—let's do our work because this window of opportunity won't last forever.

We're in 2003, and as we look out and try to grasp this opportunity, please understand—*we have power*. As a matter of fact—it's hard for you to believe this—we have more power than George Bush. We have more power! We simply have to organize it! And then take on the discipline to stick with it day after day, month after month, year after year!

Now let's go back to the 20 percent within our churches and the discipline and organization we will need. I'm really serious about this. We start with shifting our own perspective from saying, "Oh, woe is us. Our church doesn't work hard enough for peace," to "Praise God for all the thousands of people who are working!" We know we have colleagues; 20, maybe 30 percent of our congregations are really serious about peace. Perhaps it's hard for them to get organized though. Some pastors are good speakers and preachers and counselors and other things, but they're not necessarily organizers.

Our challenge now is to figure out ways in these coming years to assemble ourselves in disciplined ways. The one thing we've learned in Christian Peacemaker Teams is that when we put ourselves together and train ourselves and then sustain the work over a period of time, we can make a difference! And we are prepared to share that.

I will dare you now to think in terms of 20 percent of our congregations so well organized. I know there are criticisms of CPT, I can name them all! Nevertheless, I dare us to really get organized for active enemy loving. If we do, I promise you—now, I won't be around to have to honor this promise—there won't be future Iraqs, smart bombs will end, and the guns will go to the smelters by the end of the century. It is possible! I have been involved in many places over the years where I've seen the transformation.

There are many fronts for struggle—law, culture, health, environment, theology, to name a few. So the people around us with a diversity of gifts and callings deserve our best support. And we will naturally become more diverse than we are now because it's the only way we can do the job well.

The opening for transformation often comes when we're most discouraged. That's what we experience in CPT! Fifteen months ago, most of our people in Colombia were ordered out of the country. As I was flying there, I thought, "We're going to have to close this program and the people we have been trying to protect, some of them are going to get killed. The other stuff that we've been doing is going to come to an end and we came here and made a promise and we're not keeping our promise." That's very hard to face. And then, a kind of calmness came to my heart, because I knew—and I know from experience, it's times like this, when it feels like there is no hope, that the miracles will get started. It will happen. I promise you, it will happen. The transformation is possible.

And it's for those miracles of grace and also for the regular, well-planned work that will complement those miracles, that we are here. *We are here for such a time as this.*

A COLLEAGUE REMEMBERED

HE SOUGHT LOCAL PARTNERS ACROSS THE GLOBE

Memorial Statement Delivered at Goshen, Indiana, April 11, 2010 by CPT Co-Directors Carol Rose and Doug Pritchard

Gene Stoltzfus nurtured and shaped Christian Peacemaker Teams beginning with his presence at Techny Towers, Illinois, CPT's founding gathering, almost 25 years ago. As director for the first 16 years of CPT's organizational life, Gene's vision, ideas, and organizational initiatives laid a strong foundation for our present work. His style, faith, humor, strengths, shortcomings, and quirks are also embedded in CPT.

During Gene's tenure as director, CPT went from a dream and a dialog about more active peacemaking, to hosting the occasional short trainings and actions and to sustaining and supporting full-time field teams with hundreds of trained, active CPTers working in partnership with local peacemakers in conflict zones across the globe.

Gene's hand remains so very evident:

- in CPT's training and deployment of longer-term, diverse, disciplined, and empowered teams,
- in team and office meals and shared check ins,

- in CPT's creative direct action to reduce violence and highlight injustice,
- in patterns of prayer and mutual support to send each other out truly blessed,
- in CPT's attentiveness to exposing privilege and undoing oppression, and
- in CPT's deep roots of connection throughout the Church, which is in turn transformed into a hotbed of peacemaking.

Gene brought tremendous energy, courage, and commitment to the work of Christian peacemaking. Thank you to those who shaped his clear thinking and decisiveness—whether he practiced it challenging you and your part in holding the system in place, or you were the one who challenged him for his.

Dorothy, we thank you. Though you stepped back from public roles in CPT during the years of Gene's directorship, we recognize that your ongoing support, and your gracious strong wisdom, are also woven through CPT in ways that are very hard to differentiate from Gene's, because they were given largely through your strong support of Gene as he thought through and implemented this peacemaking initiative. You and Gene crafted your life together as a committed loving couple in a way that uniquely and intentionally freed each other up for active peacemaking.

Gene saw a military culture worldwide and asked how the church could create a counter-culture. Gene saw in us, and helped us become, competent, capable peacemakers, sharing, nurturing, and learning from many similar groups around the world. Gene held out for us a vision of a world free from war and the justifying of war. Gene successfully passed on that vision to a new generation of CPTers.

To honour Gene today, on behalf of CPT, we repeat the challenge that I'm sure you have heard before from Gene: "What are you doing to carry forward this vision of a world without war or oppression? Are you speaking the truth today? This is God calling."

I am not sure that "Rest in Peace" really fits for Gene. Perhaps he is already organizing the Celestial Peacemaker Teams. Thank-you Gene. We miss you.

HE INVITED THE CHURCHES TO A PEACE MINISTRY

Mennonite Church USA
Executive Director Ervin Stutzman

Read at the Goshen Memorial by Susan Mark Landis, Peace and Justice Minister

I am writing for Mennonite Church USA in memory of Gene Stoltzfus who served God and the church well. Since his death many people have recorded their memories of Gene. This statement reflects some of their words and themes.

As an activist, Gene was determined to bring the church with him into the trenches of peacemaking. He did not wish to create an organization disconnected from the church. With other like minded peacemakers, he invited historic peace churches to study the Bible and answer God's call to be peacemakers. Christian Peacemakers Team started as a ministry of these churches; the Steering Committee included representatives from several denominations and grants from each of them. Gene attended church conventions, stirring up people to witness against injustice, whether near the convention center or inside the church.

Gene taught us to experiment and gave us permission to fail, knowing this could lead to fresh ways to express Christian peacemaking in new contexts. He believed that disgrace came only in not trying. And if experimentation involved Santa Claus taking war toys off shelves to protect children, blowing blessed soap bubbles at ornery guards or wearing red hats to stand out in a crowd, so much the better!

Gene was a tenacious and insistent prophet who relished making people uncomfortable. But he could be pastoral, a warm and amazing listener who truly cared about people's ordinary lives. He spoke with confidence of God's will for others. He even had the audacity to impersonate God on the phone, calling someone to go on a delegation. But he was just as likely to ask how the family was doing and what was on the stove for supper.

Mennonite Church USA thanks Gene for pushing us where we thought we would never go, for providing our youth with peace heroes, for being the itch we can never reach to scratch and doing it all with humor, chocolate and ice-cream.

Gene finds inspiration in encounters with young people

THE MAN WHO CALLED ME UNCLE

By Ali Gohar, Peshawar, Pakistan
October, 2010

I met Gene when I chose to be part of a one month long non-violence course for my practicum with Christian Peacemaker Teams in Chicago. Since I was the first and only Muslim in the course, in the beginning, every one was

Gene and Ali Gohar during a CPT training in Chicago (2002)

watching me. 9/11 took place just a few months before and I was a man from Pakistan, a Pukhtoon by race, dressed in my traditional garb which people mostly saw on TV. Understandably, I was the center of attention.

Gene was thoroughly observing me. Once I took my lunch and sat in a corner to eat, as pork was on the table. He took the pork inside the kitchen asked everyone not to bring it to the table when I was there. He further asked me what I want in food and when he saw me not eating beef he inquired again. I said it was not Halal. From then on he asked everyone to bring Halal meat. I was praying in a corner so he brought a carpet for me to pray on. Similarly he brought a utensil for my ablution.

He always sat with me in eating, praying, and in non-violent action. Although I was of a different nationality and faith, he always gave me a chance to speak and share from my own faith, traditions, belief and vision.

After a week's time Gene gave feedback to some of the colleagues at Eastern Mennonite University and said, "The man is perfect." With this our friendship started.

I arranged Gene's first visit to Pakistan and Afghanistan in 2002. He learned more about my organization, *just peace international. www.justpeaceint.org.* Gene also visited Pakistan along with a team. Kathy Kelly was with him to get in-depth knowledge of the situation when the 2009 operation and drone attacks started in Pakistan and many people had to move to the Internal Displaced Persons (IDP)'s camp.

Gene created further awareness in the west through his assessments and inspirational words about the effects of western army operation, drone attacks, and the suffering and vulnerabilities of the masses. He was tirelessly writing and speaking on the issue, sharing with me and also asking for feedback.

Gene also spoke on my behalf on many occasions, mentioned my work, always called me Uncle Ali, or Uncle Alibaba. During his visit he told me, "Uncle, I will come next year on my own and will stay with you at Peshawar. As a team our visibility is much too high and an easy target to the militants." In Pakistani clothing and a cape on his head, nobody was able to recognize whether Gene was an outsider or a Pukhtoon elder.

A BROTHER REMEMBERED

By Sara Ellen Stoltzfus, Speech delivered at the Goshen, Indiana, Memorial Service April 11, 2010

In 2006 Gene wrote, *"My sojourn in the North land is proceeding with much joy. The forty years of peace work have not ended, but I've had a long discussion with myself, and with Dorothy, and have elected to enjoy this time by embracing the elements and learning to talk to the trees. I never knew how much birds, grass, snow, singing in the local Emo Centennial Choir and making twig furniture could lift the spirit and give connection to nature. The discovery that my hands can actually build something, after using my eyes, ears, mouth, and brain for forty years, has been a curious and exhilarating experience."*

It is interesting that when Gene was planning his retirement years, he returned to the trees and the woods. When our grandfather was locating a farm to buy he chose one with a marvelous stand of beech and maple trees. There is something about living trees that speaks of life and growth and gifts.

February 1, 1940. With a special twinkle in his eyes, Elmer announced to his six children, "Mother and I have a new son—another farm hand for the family farm or for one of his two farming brothers and sister." It was not long before strong, healthy Gene was biking to his assigned work area for the day or the evening chores.

Teenage years were a time of challenge. First at Aurora High School and later at Eastern Mennonite High School. The frequent letters his parents received made them wonder if they could keep up with him—much less stay ahead. Gradually Gene determined the direction he wanted his life to take.

Gene chose to live his life as a gift. He would live simply, taking every opportunity to give dignity and worth to each person or group of persons he met. There were times his family could hardly understand the decisions he was making, but nevertheless supported him—Vietnam, Washington, D.C., the Philip-

Gene at 15 months

pines, Chicago, and a good wife who wanted to keep her name—Friesen.

Often Gene would return to the woods of his childhood. The trees were now tall and majestic but were gently or cruelly being nudged to extinction to use the land for factories. As a retired gentle man he turned to the woods behind their little farmhouse near Fort Frances. He found a new harvest in the red osier dogwood, hazelnut, and willow twigs. He learned when to harvest, sort them, and keep them soft and bendable. His creative instincts and knowledgeable friends made possible surprising creations.

Early one morning last summer my doorbell rang. There was Gene looking pleased and happy. Arranged on my front porch were a gorgeous well-constructed (what he called) queen's chair with a high rounded back covered with a thick orange cushion, a footstool, a stool for the coffee cup or books, and a nice sized planter. I was delighted.

Gene was accustomed to working with problems but on this occasion one remained that he had not anticipated. There is a tight border between Canada and the United States. He had stopped at the border, uncovered his

Twig furniture made by Gene from local willow at Camp Friefus,
Off Lake, Northwestern Ontario (2009)

art work ready to be on his way when he heard the startling comment, "You cannot take those items into the US." I am sure some loud negative responses were heard.

"Give us a few minutes for discussion," he was told. After 5, 10, 20, 30 minutes and a few more questions the Ford pick-up with its twig art and bicycle were moving along the Minnesota highway. Life is a gift to be received and a gift to be shared. Only on earth does life need the earthly body. At death Gene was given the mystery of a resurrected life.

Could Gene be walking with John, the Writer? Could they be walking along the river of the water of life? Might Gene stop to observe the tree of life along the river? Stop and carefully touch the leaves, the underside, the top side, the edges? And he may be hearing the words, "The leaves of the tree are for the healing of the nations."

On March 10, much to our surprise, Gene became part of this new, yet very old, mysterious resurrection life.

Goodbye, Gene. We love you.

LOVE LETTER FOR GENE

December, 2010

Dearest Gene,

A lovely part of being given 35 years with you is that there was time to engage in the world as partners and co-workers, time to tend our relationship, time for inner work, and always the comfort of your spacious presence, whether in the same room or 10,000 miles away.

What a privilege to have been a witness and participant in your earth journey. I'm deeply grateful that neither of us left the important things unsaid; we did not fail to express our delight with each other and we did not hide our doubts. But to my surprise, coupled with the physical loss—your missing teddy bear body, booming voice, hearty chuckle, boundless enthusiasm—comes a fresh perspective of our shared terrain, now in sharper focus and through a wider aperture.

I remember a late summer trip some years ago, one of the many from Canada to Chicago in your little dark blue truck, roll-up windows and no air conditioning. It is at a time when we are each facing external circumstances that challenge and affect our relationship. You stare straight ahead, all attention on the road. "Do you think I understand you?" I ask. We watch hundreds of majestic pines, shoulder to shoulder, slip by along the two lane highway. Finally you say, "Yes, as much as someone can."

"Do you think you understand me?" I ask. Many miles of silence. "No" you say, finally. More silence. Then the truck slows and pulls onto the shoulder. You look at me with those big brown eyes and say with a fervor usually reserved for rallying people to put their bodies on the line for peace. "But I know I love you."

I, who have always trusted problems could be resolved by a more articulate statement or cogent explanation, am startled into silence.

Years earlier we also sat side by side, a table rather than a windshield in front of us, at Church Community Services where I worked, and where you, as the director of the national Mennonite Voluntary Service, placed volunteers. It was late February, 1975 and we were addressing our home designed wedding invitations that featured a spreading tree with tangled roots and Gandhi's words:

"Truth is like a vast tree, which yields more and more fruit the more you nurture it. The deeper the search in the mine of truth the richer the discovery of the gems buried there, in the shape of openings for an ever greater variety of service."

A phone call came from your anti-war colleagues in Washington, DC asking you to accompany a congressional delegation to Vietnam to introduce them to real Vietnamese people's concerns about the US-funded war. You had left DC in 1972, a conscious decision to shift your work for peace from the halls of political power to the grass roots church base. But the stakes were high.

When Gene was preparing to marry Dorothy during a period when I was living in India, he responded to my invitation for wedding gift ideas with a humble request for a Gandhian homespun cotton kurta. I was honored to send him this symbol of non-violent advocacy and to learn that he had worn it for the wedding ceremony.

- John Sommer, Dummerston, Vermont

Your friends were already known to the CIA and their operatives in Vietnam. You still knew your way around the country, you spoke the language, you were the person to go.

Your going to Vietnam confirmed our marriage goals of coming together for "an ever greater variety of service." You would surely be back before April 4th, the date printed on our invitation. However, when the congressional delegation prolonged their fact finding trip in order to investigate the US bombings of Cambodia, I became concerned. Should I postpone the wedding, find a proxy for the day, or just hope for the best? But you managed to breeze into Elkhart's tiny airport with no visible jet lag and penned the wedding welcome statement that, in retrospect, I see as your maxim for life.

Gene and Dorothy's Wedding Welcome Statement

This is an excerpt from the welcome Gene wrote for his and Dorothy's marriage ceremony on April 4, 1975 at the Chapel of the Sermon on the Mount at the Associated Mennonite Biblical Seminaries.

Our celebration… with one another and before God will have integrity if we acknowledge at the outset the brokenness that exists in so many places where a community of justice has not yet been achieved… Let us remember these visible objective wounds… Let us also acknowledge that much of this brokenness begins and is nourished in our own lives. But let us recall that God's grace is most visible in the presence of such brokenness.

May this time together be a celebration of our faith and hope for the future because we know that the reality of new life, tenderness and love, is struggling at this moment to be freed and to be made real.

You have been driving steadily, and by now the solid green conifers are giving way to quaking aspen, ash and white trunk birch trees. I sneak a glance at the driver's seat, at you who love me; your one hand is on the wheel, legs stretched out, thanks to cruise control, the one luxurious necessity.

I know your soft heart. I also know the visible wounds of the world, the personal disappointments and your own shadow wrestling have striated that tender organ, and probably left a few deep indentations as well. But each morning, heart cracked wide open, you get out of bed and engage with life, your eye on the as-yet invisible prize—a world without war. That you do this without numbing your feelings amazes me. To stay on point and vulnerable day after day, year after year, without resorting to rose colored glasses takes as much courage as standing in front of a million tanks and guns.

Some of that soul muscle you surely developed through praxis over the years, but you must have arrived on earth, as William Wordsworth wrote, your "life's Star, ...trailing clouds of glory." However, unlike the poet's prediction that "shades of the prison-house ...close upon the growing Boy," you resisted attempts to constrict your free spirit. I loved your childhood story about an overly pious adult who tried to keep your rowdiness in check. Pushed to the brink one day, you responded with a defiant, "damn you," completely inappropriate words for a minister's son. You accepted your punishment and then crept to the chicken coop to meet your Maker. "If this is how you work, you'll just have to damn me to hell," you told God. "Because this is how I am." Bravo, eight year old child. You pierced the mirage of the punishing god, created by the sanctimonious who fashion that god in their own image to control others.

Using an earthier idiom than the poet, your dairy farmer nephew told me, "Gene could smell a pile of manure a mile away." We may all possess a built-in "crap meter" as your nephew calls it, but unlike many of us, you trusted yours and calibrated it finely. That enabled you to assess events and situations quickly and see through sophisticated blather with surety. I confess it took me some time to recognize your gift, and even longer to appreciate how patiently you waited for me to tune my own meter.

> Dear Dorothy People knit a prayer shawl especially for you and prayed on it in the Newton office of Mennonite Church USA (where Gene worked in Mennonite Voluntary Service) at a Newton area peace meting and at the CPT Steering Committee meeting in March, where we all touched it and prayed for you.
>
> - *Susan Mark Landis, Mennonite Church USA*

But I believe that you, the child of a community and family of farmers, had a head start. The generations were grounded in hard work, yet yearly they experienced that the fruit of their labor was at the mercy of the seasons. Deep in the communal bones they, and through them, you, understood that both the work and the grace of good weather, something beyond human control, are needed for success. I admired the disciplined work habits that had you at the CPT office by six in the morning to do the computer work so you could be freer during the day to greet the guests and have time for deeper conversations. You continued those disciplined habits in retirement with six pans of bread dough mixed and kneaded and rising in the oven before I even woke up.

You surely imbibed your father's blend of pastoral presence and friendly curiosity about the wider world, and your mother's warm hospitality that always included food for anyone who came to the door. As youngest child, you were influenced and nourished by the conversations and actions of older brothers and sisters, whether or not they were directed at you.

Brother Glenn, seven years older, spent hours pulling you around the farmyard, and teaching you the guilty pleasure of sneaking to the basement freezer with a serving spoon to dip ice cream right out of the gallon size pail. Brother Ed returned from college to challenge the decision to call the police when the house was burgled. You were impressed with your father's willingness to discuss the finer points of co-operation with the various expressions of the state's use of force. Brother Bob, fifteen years older, took

Stoltzfus family picture, taken 1969. Back row (left to right) brothers Bob, Dwight, Gene, Glenn, Ed. Front row (left to right) Sara Ellen, Father Elmer, Mother Orpha Beechy, Evelyn

a cattle boat to Poland after the second world war to help in the agricultural rebuilding there, and sparked in you the possibilities of service overseas. Sara, your sister and friend, supported you in so many ways throughout life, and surely her example of no-nonsense empathy must have nurtured your positive feelings toward women and the feminine within you. Oldest sister Evelyn and her family provided a relaxed atmosphere and laughter whenever you, as a young boy, helped with chores on their farm. Brother Dwight, twenty years your senior became a colleague later in life and engaged you in animated conversations about church and political issues. I will never forget standing beside Dwight's truck at the edge of a hayfield, perhaps one of the last times he drove a vehicle. He faced you straight on, placed his hands on your upper arms and said, "I am so proud of you, Gene. Our little brother Gene."

What you were given, you passed on—an inquiring mind, an example of service, laughter, hospitality, encouragement and support—not only to biological nieces and nephews and their children, but to any members of the human family you encountered. You took joy in spotting people's talents and providing opportunities and sometimes pushing them to develop and use their abilities. I clearly remember the bright sunny afternoon when you thrust a camera into my hand near our Davao City squatter home and insisted I take pictures, this after months of my own insisting that I was not technically able. How thankful I am that you pushed.

A hundred miles have passed silently as the meaning of your simple words, "But I know I love you," filter through my brain and sink into my heart, like gentle snowflakes silently filling the tiny crevices of a rock. Amid the vicissitudes of life—betrayal, heart break, disappointment—no matter how hard I try to correct the situation, the roads of rational explanation lead to a dead end. You, on the other hand, trust each moment as it appears and give yourself fully to it. Somehow in that acceptance you learned to make love your default position.

I pour the last drops from the stainless steel thermos into your cup. It will soon be my time to take the wheel. Finally I say, "Gene, you don't understand, but you love? That's profound, actually." You reply without missing a beat.

"Right. Though I wasn't sure you'd realize that." Your eyes are twinkling. We both laugh.

In the early years of marriage, I did not always recognize the depth from which you worked, and you rarely wasted time explaining. For you, words were flotsam carried by the underground river of life, slippery approximations of where and how fast the stream may be flowing. You preferred to dip directly into the river, drawing the water of life through the particular well entrusted to you, but never confusing the well, the enclosed form needed to make the water accessible, with the wild river itself.

Gene, my faithful and wise traveling companion over water and land, I thank you and the Universe from the bottom of my heart. It's been a grand ride.

Always,

Dorothy

March 10, 2000

WORTH LIVING FOR, WORTH DYING FOR

Wednesday, March 10, 2010

This is Gene's last essay, completed on Wednesday, March 10, 2010, just before heading out on his beloved motor-assisted bicycle on the first spring-like day of the year. He picked up his mail in International Falls, Minnesota. Then on his return, less than a kilometer from home, he serenely rode into God's embrace.

I have talked to survivors of military interrogation around the world who at some point thought they would not live for another day. I never write about it in the US and Canada because it seems so unbelievable and out of place in a world of shopping malls and super highways. When I retell their stories I notice that people here fidget. Interrogation processes are one way in which martyrs are surfaced in our world, but martyrs are truly created by a deep commitment of conscience that sustains them through moments of cruelty and abuse.

In our time the word martyr has morphed from its root meaning of "witness to the truth" to a description of someone who dies for his or her beliefs. The Greeks and early Christians who used the term understood death to be a possible outcome of the path to truth and light. Eventually the word martyr referred exclusively to those who died for their belief. Those who began as witnesses to truth became martyrs at the time of death. For the Muslim, shahada (martyrdom) also springs from the internal struggle that results in the witness to truth. In today's times of political conflict and triumphalism, both the Christian and Muslim traditions have departed from the core understanding of martyrdom.

Some martyrs are killed during interrogation. They never get to tell the story. So I have learned to listen to those who narrowly avoid that brush with death.

In the late 1970s when I worked in the Philippines, I was invited to meet a pastor and former political prisoner. The Marcos dictatorship had sent its military and paramilitary to his community and he felt bound by his convictions to do what was possible to protect the people of his church. The military tactics were designed to control popular discontent through cruelty, terror, domination, killing, and confiscation of property. The pastor was arrested and interrogated for weeks. His body was spent. Finally he was blindfolded and told he would be killed. He felt the barrel of a revolver that touched the temple of his head and rested there for a time while his interrogator demanded that he give names of the people with whom he worked. "I was silent because I couldn't think any more," he told me.

"Were you afraid you would endanger others?" I asked. "Of course I was worried that I might implicate others but when the gun was put to my head, I really couldn't think of anything to say. I was ready to die. I just told them to get it over with. The interrogator didn't pull the trigger. I don't know why."

In 2003 I spent two hours in Iraq talking to a 22-year-old student who was arrested in a house raid along with two of his brothers. Until the time of his capture he was relatively uninvolved politically, not an unusual story in the Iraq of that time. After his capture by American military personnel he was not allowed to sleep for two days. After 48 hours the American GIs told him that he would be killed unless he told them where Saddam Hussein was hiding. He was kept blindfolded. He was told that his brother, taken into custody at the same time, was just now being shot. In the distance he could hear a gun being fired. If he didn't want to die, he must tell all. Then he heard a gun being cocked and felt a revolver touching his head. There was more shouting from the soldiers and then silence.

"I believed I would die," he told me. "And then after a long wait I felt my hand to be sure I was still alive." His blindfold was temporarily removed and then he was marched off to one of Iraq's prison camps. There he met others who experienced similar beatings and moments of terror. He was released three months later because of persistent outside intervention— an advantage that many disappeared people do not have.

> Soon after Gene's memorial service, our 4 year old Elias said,
>
> "Mama, I love Gene Stoltzfus. But he died."
>
> "Yeah, he died, sweetie."
>
> "But he's still in our bodies, right? And if he's in our bodies,
> That means he's still alive, right?"
>
> "Right, Sweetie!"
>
> *Sent by parents, Mark Frey and Sara Reschly, Chicago, Illinois*

After my talk with the unlikely martyr, I pondered the connection of this Muslim student to my own ancestors in 16th century Europe. Death by burning or drowning is now little practiced, but current authorities still believe that truth can be accessed by means of brutality. Why are soldiers and interrogators still trained in the craft of torture? Why do Christian crusaders or Muslim suicide bombers slip into patterns of domination that kill and destroy in a manner that cannot possibly reveal truth?

Martyrs have all the foibles of the rest of us. Some may not deserve the label. But, in our human family, great movements that push us to transcend boundaries with visions of hope, produce martyrs. However, those same movements can be undercut when they protect themselves too much from the risk of great witness and possible martyrdom.

The test of true martyrs is whether they sustain their community's commitment to a full-bodied vision of peace and justice. They are with us, and may be more powerful for their witness in death than they ever could have been in life.

Gene reads the Martyr's Mirror, The Netherlands (2009)

FAREWELL

Excerpts from Gene's River Reflections and his farewell letter to the CPT community when he retired in September 2004

My work here is finished.

With you I have lived out my deepest convictions in the great experiment of love-making on this planet. I have tried to create forms that carry the spirit of nonviolence when engaging in experiments of truth. I have strived to build an organization where power and influence was dispersed, and structures of fair decision-making allowed for maximum flexibility and quick response. I have tried to join in creating a place where laughter was expected, ceremony made common and worship was welcome. I have tried to prepare us to be a worldwide power of Christian peacemaking.

We have grown together. We have been changed. Together we have passed through life and death crises. Among you I have learned how to listen to the voice of the Spirit and have been surprised and astonished at how we have been sustained.

As I go I will hold you in prayer, in that spot where the mystery of the universe holds us all together in a unity of purpose and imagination. I know that the great Spirit will bless and keep you in new and profound ways that we cannot expect to envision at this time.

Thank you for letting me be with you in this way. And thank you for letting me participate for a brief moment in the work of transformation.

At the Roman Garden in Chester, UK, during a speaking tour in January, 2009

There is a River

There is a magnificent river that flows gently at times, powerfully at others. Its waters are mysteriously composed of two parts hydrogen, and one part oxygen. Between these two elements the universal Spirit that connects everywhere holds the atoms together to support the one mystery of the universe.

Amidst gigantic dangerous cliffs the river winds its way to the sea. Pure, clean water in that river—enough to quench the deep thirst in all the animals and plants and people. Even the great machines cannot destroy the river.

The River flows on...

In the midst of that river I see a collection of rocks, proud and confident in their majesty. I see a big rock whose size and form challenge the great boulders to notice. One small sandstone rock worries that no one will notice it. A granite rock appears to have been erected in that place at the beginning of eternity. Wide furrows of water are created as the river parts in its meeting with the granite.

And the River flows on...

One tiny rock reminds the others every day that there is danger threatening in the great cliffs. The rocks call out to the cliffs that line the river to overcome their temptation to plunge into the water and block the great river's course. But year after year the rocks continue to grace the river as beautiful compositions of history.

And the River flows on...

And the great Spirit that no one could find hidden between the two parts of hydrogen and the one part oxygen is very happy with the rocks. When the wind and rain retreat there is a melody that sounds like it might be great blessing.

And the River flows on...

One day the rocks have a great gathering. And there is disagreement. Some rocks think that they should be organized differently. Some think there should be no organization. Other rocks think it should be just like it always was. Some feel that there should be many, many different kinds of rocks. And the river continues to flow. After the disagreement there is great love among the rocks. Even the rocks in the cliff are surprised.

And the River flows on...

The sound of the Spirit in the river becomes more beautiful. And the rocks think there will be peace. But just when it seems like the peace is near there is a storm. Huge boulders plunge into the river. The beautiful community of rocks is dislodged. Some are pushed down river and buried. Others are submerged in the torrent. A few try to hold back the powerful boulders from the cliff so that the river can flow. Anguish, suspicion, and confusion envelop the valley. Some wonder if the great Spirit of the river has abandoned them and that eternity has been broken.

And the River flows on...

And then the great storm is over. The boulders have been stopped by some unyielding power in the river of timelessness. The rocks glisten in the sun with an illumination that restores a new majesty to the great valley. And love returns and the rocks look kindly after each other. And the music of the Spirit in the river can be heard in the distance beyond the cliffs and mountains and some say even to the islands of the distant sea.

And the River flows on...

The rocks discern that all that exists downstream will be changed in great and subtle ways for they have all been touched by the Spirit of the river. And the rocks realize that together they are helping to shape the course of the river.

And the River flows on...

ADDENDUM

After Gene's death, thoughts, poems, remembrances of Gene, and expressions of hope for creating space for peace arrived from the world over. We share excerpts from the many messages received, arranged in categories that echo the four sections of the book.

... SHINING THE LIGHT

Gene helped me figure out what role I should be playing as a Mennonite Central Committee volunteer in Vietnam in the '70s. He also encouraged me to write about what I saw in Vietnam, the Philippines, and Laos, which eventually resulted in my spending over 20 years as a journalist writing about God's favorite continent.

—*Murray Hiebert, Senior Director, Asia Policy, US Chamber of Commerce, Washington, DC*

I remember one meeting in a restaurant during the middle years of the war when Gene, on home leave from Vietnam told me about the real situation, saying that we are not on the side of the people there. He was responsible for my becoming active in anti-Vietnam war activities.

—*Marion G. Bontrager, Biblical Studies and Theology, Hesston College, Hesston, Kansas*

I met Gene in Vietnam, He has helped me learn many things, including the idea that one can forge one's own destiny if one tries hard enough. I am a stronger, hopefully more loving person for having known Gene.

—*Tom Fox, National Catholic Reporter, Kansas City*

I'll remember Gene warmly as the exuberant youth who starred in the International Voluntary Services film that Dave Colyer and I made in 1964.

—*Phyllis Westover, Kansas City, Missouri*

Gene was someone who made people uncomfortable in important ways. He never tired of raising issues of justice, and partnered, with respect, across generations. As a young woman leader I was empowered by him to use my voice courageously. His parting words to me as I joined the Mennonite Church USA staff: "Don't let them water you down."

—*Joanna Shenk, Elkhart, Indiana*

Ever since Gene and I "bonded" at a Service Order retreat and took puffs from a cigar, I've felt like a friend. And this friendship was renewed in 2009 at the court trial regarding crossing the line at Fort McCoy, Wisconsin where troops are trained for house to house search and destroy missions in Iraq. I remember also that we had a line crossing in Wichita at the McConnell Air Force Base in protest against the B1 bombers.

—*Tom Haebig, West Bend, Wisconsin*

Gene

In the summer of 1983
At the height of martial law
In the Philippines, I worked with him
In Synapses, Chicago.
There he made me feel
A member of his own family.
He made me feel strong
In the midst of threats
Of arrest and torture.
His commitment to our cause
Made me courageous,
Strong enough to pursue
Human rights work.
He has a soft heart
Like that of a woman.
As a friend, I felt comfortable
And safe with him,
He was a big sister
And brother all in one.
His last visit to the Philippines
Was a trip down memory lane
In my neighborhood
He walked around like he had
Never left the place.

—*Myrna Arceo, Batangas City, Philippines*

Gene was fun to be around even when it was serious. I remember from our CPT trip to Haiti in 1992. We had gone to meet a group ...After we had talked with the person in charge, he gave us a tour of the place and then led us to a door that opened onto an empty field, and the guy said, "And this is where we will build the clinic/school/etc. that you are going to fund for us."... It was assumed that we were a group with a lot of money to hand out. I was standing next to Gene. Gene just pointed to me and said, "Talk to him, he is the one with the money." Gene took several steps away, and left me standing there open-mouthed... I still laugh at that experience.

—*J. Denny Weaver, Madison, Wisconsin*

With the limited time we had together, I found Gene a deeply caring person, conversant with so many subjects and thoughtful of many. He had the ability to bridge worlds very quickly, to reach out.

—*Meral Muratkhan, Lahore, Pakistan*

The two of us loved cooking. Bishop Gene—I called him my Bishop and he called me his pastor—would cook his favorite Vietnamese dishes with fish sauce, and whenever I visited him, he always requested my adobo del rey specialty. My friendship with Gene spanned years of peace organizing—in Chicago where we worked together in Synapses for several years, in urban organizing in DC to close a crack house, during the embargo on Haiti where we went to Port Jeremie to accompany the parishioners of St. Helen, in the struggles of the Canadian First Nations people for their fishing rights in Burnt Church, New Brunswick, in the exploratory trip and the first CPT Peace delegation in the Philippines, and most recently October 2009 when he and Dorothy hosted me in their home in Fort Frances, Ontario, after I joined the CPT delegation in Kenora, Canada. I will miss cooking adobo for my beloved friend and peace mentor.

—*Rey Lopez, Parañaque, Philippines*

I first met Gene in the late 1960's when he left Vietnam and together we visited many key members of Congress to tell the Truth about the war in Vietnam. Then in early 90's Gene started CPT and I co-founded the Nonviolent Peaceforce. Gene and I last talked a few days before he died when I was trying to decide whether to go to trial for my arrest in protesting the Drones at the Creech Air Force Base near Las Vegas where we were both arrested last September. Gene encouraged me to call him anytime when discerning big questions like this. Unfortunately, it will be harder to get Gene's advice on future projects unless I tune in very well.

Gene was planning to go back to Creech Air Force Base in Nevada for a couple weeks the end of March, 2010 to explore a more sustained nonviolent campaign there and he encouraged me to come along. He had also hoped to go back to Pakistan to further explore what role the peace movement could play to help prevent further escalation of the Afghanistan war into Pakistan. I trust that many of us will continue the good and hard work where Gene left off.

—*David Hartsough, Founder, Non-Violent Peaceforce, California*

Gene will travel with us as we head over to Pakistan. Gene's thoughts about the necessity to take risks on behalf of deepened understanding, guided a trip to Pakistan one year ago. We are very fortunate to feel, in the deep heart's core, that we are still all part of one another.

—*Kathy Kelly, Voices for Creative Non-Violence, Chicago, Illinois*

For all the serious and important work that Gene has done he never took himself seriously. His smiles, his laughter, his sense of humor drew us to the cause of peace because we could see that we did not need to be dour and humorless to work for peace. His blog on the use of torture and cruel interrogation really hit home to me. On that same evening in Baghdad when he was recording the story of one of those brothers who was tortured, I was doing the same with another of the brothers.

Gene followed his heart, used all his skills and imagination to work for a more just and peaceful world.

—*Allan Slater, Lakeside, Ontario*

Dorothy and Gene have had a profound impact on my life, and I am deeply appreciative. I still remember clearly standing on the sidewalk of Cullerton Street in the Pilsen community in Chicago, and Gene enthusiastically telling me about the community organizing in Nicaragua he'd seen on the first Witness for Peace delegation there, and encouraging me to see it for myself.

Going to Central America, helping at Synapses with computer, carting embargoed Nicaraguan coffee around the city, singing coffee hymns, meeting activists from around the world at these great Synapses lunches—all of these things involved me in a community of struggle and set a direction for my life.

It was great to participate with Gene in the men's group. He pushed us to share more deeply with each other. He also instigated a lot of fun. I know I'm one of many who felt Gene's joy in who we are and our unique contributions to the cause.

— *Lauren Martens, Denver Colorado*

Gene was one of the most unforgettable "Merkano" males I've ever met . He was sincere and strong and simple in living his principles even at the risk of harm. I'm very thankful our lives crossed paths even for only a few years...

— *Agnes Miclat, Davao City, Philippines*

Gene's stay and work in Mindanao, though brief, contributed in the shaping of lay empowerment and work for justice in those dark days of Martial Law in the Philippines. I am one of the "oldies" from the Muslim-Christian dialogue of the Archdiocese of Cotabato during the peak days of the Mindanao Sulu Pastoral Conference in the 70s. We deeply mourn his passing...

— *Rev Fr. Eliseo "Jun" Mercado, OMI Cotabato, Philippines*

It was 20 plus years ago when I first met Gene and Dorothy. Each time I went to the Synapses House for a meeting or an event my time was prolonged by at least an additional hour. Our conversations were intense and even though we agreed on many things, there were lots of different opinions. That never interrupted a friendship. Gene had lots of questions about race and how to approach the conversation in Synapses initially and then later with CPT.

I remember a call I got from Gene some years ago about going on a trip with him to Afghanistan. Given the gender issues there it was necessary to have a woman who could speak to women and develop a deeper gender understanding. At the time I made lots of excuses as to why I couldn't go, but I was really scared. I didn't have the courage. I've regretted my decision since then.

Gene always challenged me to think outside of myself. I will always remember his dedication and his courage.

— *Mary Scott-Boria, Chicago, Illinois*

… PRACTICING PEACEMAKING

Gene will be extremely missed by the Peace Community far and wide . What a witness the two of you are. He joined us here April 2009 for the Space Symposium demonstration, a special gift…

— *Esther Leatherman Kisamore, Bijou Community and Citizens for Peace in Space, Colorado*

I knew Gene since the CPT Techny consultation in 1986. Just over a year ago I sat with him at the kitchen table at my home. We talked about getting CPT involvement in The Netherlands. He was a great help in that starting phase. His presence in congregations and a conference showed a rare mix of empathy, humor and personal conviction. For each audience he had a special way to approach dialogue. This example will stay with me as a guiding image of how to work for peace.

He writes in his last essay about the Martyrs Mirror, how important it was for him. I remember looking with him through an original Martyrs Mirror and how a deep atmosphere of respect and reflection was present.

— *Maarten van der Werf, CPT support group Netherlands.*

When Gene was director of Mennonite Voluntary Service in the 70s he recommended I read The Last Western by Thomas Klis. It told of a compassionate radical Christian religious order called The Silent Servants of the Used,

Abused and Utterly Screwed Up which gave unpredictable self-sacrificing help to people in trouble. That eccentric group fit Gene's life, sense of humor, and the creativity he gave to Christian Peacemaker Teams.

— *Stan Bohn, Newton Kansas*

Besides being a tremendous embodiment of peace-building and prophetic witness, Gene was an important influence in my life—giving me tangible support at a time when I was just beginning to compose music. When he was director of Mennonite Voluntary Service (MVS) back in the '70s, he encouraged me to record my first album of music and MVS underwrote the cost of its production. As a young adult (in my twenties) I was grateful, but now in retrospect, I realize what a remarkable risk that was! And that album gave me confidence to pursue further musical projects!

— *Patty Shelly, Professor of Bible and Religion,* Bethel College, Newton, Kansas

I met both Gene and Dorothy at a formative time in my life. As a restless, idealistic teenager, a volunteer in Mennonite Voluntary Service, I was deeply affected by Gene's approach to life. Knowing him helped shape my values and the choices I have made over the years.

Gene was passionate about his beliefs yet never judgmental, deeply dedicated to putting words to action, yet always ready to laugh and celebrate the lighter moments, and most of all, sweet and loving and faithful to friends and family.

— *Ruth Teichroeb*, Seattle, Washington

The news of Gene's death hit me like lightning. We had worked together in the 80s and for a peace witness on the site of nuclear weapons in North Dakota at the time of the Mennonite World Conference Winnipeg Assembly 1990. I loved his wit and his commitment. Now that Gene is no longer present on this side, we need many more to witness for peace and to get in the way for the sake of peace and justice. What can we say other than "Presente!" and not rest but live in peace.

— *Hansulrich Gerber*, Berne, Switzerland

Through the years, Gene and Dorothy have inspired our community of friends—justice and peace workers everyone—to "let justice roll like raging waters" even as we walk the way of peace. I feel that the "seed" of Christian Peacemakers Team blossomed among us, "Filipino style." I'm sure you can visualize and appreciate the variety of expressions of that "style." My heart feels the pain of Gene's loss from our midst but I also celebrate his LIFE.

— *Jeannette Birondo, New York*

Just a little over a year ago Gene came to our community in Groningen, the Netherlands. He inspired us with his realistic idealism. Peace is difficult but it can be done! And it can be done not only by some but by everyone. This is the essence of believe and hope.

— **Geert Brusewitz,** *Netherlands*

A memory I cherish of Gene and Dorothy was the afternoon we shared in their Chicago apartment. Gene reflected on his recent time in Iraq. I was deeply touched by his concern for each person and his nonviolent efforts to make a difference. I hope that my current efforts regarding systems change in Illinois for women and children are as compassionate and caring.

— **Rose Mary Meyer,** *BVM Chicago IL*

I remember the first time Gene came to join The Emo Centennial Choir. His presence was both so strong and gentle at the same time.

— **Renée Martin-Brown, Choir Director,** *Emo, Ontario*

I spoke with Gene on the telephone shortly before he died. He was his usual energetic quirky perky witty prophetic activist self. "Are you speaking the truth?" he asked me, in that frank get-right-down-to-the-heart-of-the-matter way of his, a twinkle in his voice. I hadn't talked to him for several years, so the directness of the question, in that between-friends way, was both startling and lovely, intimate, refreshing.

— **Di Brandt, Canada Research Chair in Literature and Creative Writing,** *Brandon University, Brandon, Manitoba*

A few of the pieces that made up the mosaic life of Gene:

When Gene traveled to Afghanistan, Pakistan, Haiti, Iraq or the West Bank, he went to places where people were suffering.

When he walked near his home at Friefus Place, he had his eyes open for particular reeds that could be used to make twig furniture.

When he ate at the Nile restaurant, he would greet the owner in Arabic.

When he sat on our screen porch and told stories, I felt he was in a sacred space.

When he was in the Cook County Hospital for surgery, he blended in with the others with whom he shared the dorm-style room

Last summer, I listened for hours as he and an old friend shared stories from the days when they played a role in changing how Congress viewed the Vietnam War.

When he checked in by phone with Dorothy at the end of the day, he was like a teenager who had just fallen in love.

Through his blog, he reflected on the events of the day with decades of understanding of peacemaking.

He attracted attention when he rode his amazing motor assisted bicycle hundreds of miles.

He connected with the local Ojibwa people as he made earrings out of bones and antlers found near his home.

When he ate pancakes with real maple syrup, he paid particular attention to the taste.

But I know that I've seen only a tiny part of the mosaic.

— *Dale Fast*, *Chicago, Illinois*

Our deep and sincere condolences for the passing of a great friend, Gene Stoltzfus. He was a great inspiration for us in Bethlehem.

— *Zoughbi Zoughbi, Founder & Director The Palestinian Conflict Resolution Centre, "WI'AM"-Bethlehem*

Gene was very much a part of the CPT Iraq story from the beginning. He directed, supported, and cherished our ministry of peace in this conflicted land. We held a memorial for him in Iraq joining our prayers to those in Canada and elsewhere.

— *The CPT Iraq Team, Chichun Yaun, Michele Naar-Obed, Zack Selekman, Bob Holmes*

We both thought of Gene as a dear friend and a challenging role model. What a gift he was to the world! What a life—and on the first spring-like day of his seventieth year, he rode his bike right into eternity!

— *Liz and Perry Yoder, Ely, Minnesota*

Gene was such an encourager of my work. I tended to feel young and inexperienced in my ministry and Gene has always supported me, made me feel as if what I was doing was worthwhile and challenging me to go even further, having the confidence that I could. What a privilege to be in the same family with him.

— *Cindy Lapp, Pastor, Hyattsville Mennonite Church, Maryland*

Gene's voice was so far ahead of the time, his readiness to see war for what it was. My memory of Gene is one of appreciation for the courage and clarity he brought to each day.

— *Bert Lobe, St. Jacob's, Ontario*

For those who didn't have the honor of meeting Gene, we hope someday, somewhere his peace legacy will be recognized and appreciated in terms of following the peace journey he took.

— *Ed de la Torre and Girlie Villariba, Manila*

We thank Gene for his life, his light, and his presence. May the seeds of peace that he planted in his life finally bear fruit.

    — *Liza Almojuela, BodyTalk Philippines*

Gene will always be remembered as one shining light, a peacebuilder, peace maker, peacekeeper. Blessed are those whose life he had touched.

    — *Chic S. Ramoso, Davao, Philippines*

I would describe Gene as brave, bold, and brilliant, but what he was in person was humble, sweet, and lovable, and that is the enduring memory. I know he witnessed in war zones, listened to interrogation survivors, helped people search for their disappeared loved ones—that he touched thousands through CPT—but what I will remember most is his delicious bread, his gorgeous twig furniture and tree and bone earrings, his infectious laugh, and his deep love for Dorothy.

He embodied those aphorisms we love to quote: "the personal is political" and "be the change you wish to see in the world." It may be that, as Gene wrote in his last blog, his "witness will be more powerful in death even than in life." Adelante!

    — *Bonnie Bazata, Director, Bridges out of Poverty, South Bend, Indiana*

I'd like to thank God for having had the opportunity of meeting Gene last year in Berlin. He was an inspiration for my congregation, and for my work.

    — *Martina Basso, Director of the Mennonite Peacecenter of Berlin and Pastor of the Berlin Mennonite Congregation, Germany*

Gene came to my life as a surprise, I am the richer in many ways. He called us "co-confessors"—and I knew I could speak in full honesty with him. Gene drew me into contact with a world I'd only heard of and he made it real to me. Lunch was shared at the only restaurant in International Falls that could cater to tastes he acquired in Vietnam and the Philippines. I could only handle the tiniest portion of the pepper sauce he used there with great delight.

On the day I heard of his death I went and had egg rolls dipped in his pepper sauce, and through my tears finding to my amazement the wonderful flavors which he always knew were hidden in the sauce. Wonderful flavors are hidden in the pains, joys, sorrows, and comforts of this life, and I thank God for opening my experience of them through his presence in Gene.

— *Marty Wenger, International Falls, Minnesota*

It was already 8 p.m. when I left Emo, Ontario and the Memorial service for Gene and I had more than a 6-hour drive ahead of me to St. John's Abbey in Minnesota that night. But the Spirit provided other unexpected opportunities. When I got to the US border at International Falls, the border agent looked at my passport and asked the usual questions. Then she handed my passport to another agent who took some time to do a computer search. She also searched the trunk. Then she asked me to pull off to the side and come inside. There I was handed over to another US Customs agent who asked me to take a seat and spent a long time with my passport and the computer. Finally he asked me to come over and to take my jacket off and empty my pockets and turn them inside-out. He began asking many questions until he finally got to his real interest: Iraq. When were you in Iraq? How did you get a visa? Why were you there? Who was with you? Who did you see?

I got to tell a lot of the Rutba story to a very skeptical agent. "Do you have a church in Rutba?" "No, we were visiting Iraqi Muslims." "Oh," he said seemingly relieved," so you were converting Muslims?" "No, we were meeting with Iraqi people who had saved our lives so we could thank them and continue telling the story." None of it made sense to him. Finally he asked, "How did you get a visa?" I said, "Because God opened the door to an Iraqi Ambassador who thought our mission was a noble one and gave us visas." "No," he said, "I don't mean Iraq. I mean our country. How did our country let you do this?" "We didn't ask permission from our country, but we did have a very interesting meeting with Captain Foster, the head US military officer at the Iraq border."

Utterly baffled and conveying clearly that he thought there had to be something wrong with this picture, he was determined to keep me for a long time. I had lots of opportunity to tell him what it means to follow Jesus and to be Mennonite, a pastor, and a peacemaker. Finally the agent asked me to be seated and disappeared for sometime and then returned with another agent.

We went through the whole baffled skeptical Q&A again. Meanwhile the first agent went out and searched my car. Finally, they returned my passport, thanked me for my time, and said I was free to go on the way.

Something struck me as I drove away. I was in Canada because our beloved friend and mentor Gene Stoltzfus had died much too young and quickly when we still longed for his humor, wisdom, friendship, and inspiring peacemaking witness in the church and in the world. Nevertheless, I could just imagine Gene looking down with great amusement and saying, "Weldon, why didn't you invite them to join you for ice cream after they finished asking you questions?" I can hear him say it!

— *Weldon Nisly, Pastor, Seattle Mennonite Church, Seattle, Washington*

Gene was a person that by his actions helped me have faith in the Christian faith. When it was easy to write off Christians and Christianity for not following Jesus, Gene helped show that it was possible.

— *Richard Rutschman, Chicago, Ilinois*

Gene and I went to Vietnam together in 1963 with International Voluntary Services. Our initial assignment was to establish hamlet schools, he in a coastal province some four hours from my highland posting. We exchanged periodic visits to compare notes and share good cheer, and in 1965 we were both promoted to be team leaders, shortly after which our sharings became clouded by the increasing Americanization and escalation of the war and the increasing misery it inflicted on the Vietnamese people.

Gene has often cited his Vietnam experience as profoundly influencing his future course, not only in fighting for peace in that country but, through the amazing work of CPT, throughout the world. I treasure the chance he and I had to spend a month in Vietnam again in 2009, his first post-war visit, and a moving one, indeed.

— *John Sommer, Dummerston, Vermont*

Remembering Our Brother Gene

By Don Goertzen

A cross-section of the Filipino family of Gene Stoltzfus and Dorothy Friesen gathered on a warm Monday morning, March 15, at the Religious of the Good Shepherd chapel in Quezon City for a Memorial Mass to celebrate the life and spirit of their departed brother Gene.

Set in front of the altar was a framed photograph of Gene: full grey beard, impish smile, and eyes twinkling as people remembered him. A spray of white and yellow sunflowers, candles and paper peace cranes adorned the simple display.

The mass was officiated in English by Fr.Efren Borromeo and Fr. Gil of the Healing Ministry. Familiar songs in Tagalog brought the congregation of over a 100 to their feet. During prayer and song people's eyes darted left and right. Some of the congregants were regularly in touch with each other at church events, NGO meetings, Body Talk and healing sessions, or for other events. Some were less familiar... "Is that... yes, just add ten, or twenty years."

Fr. Efren Borromeo officiates at Memorial Mass in Quezon City, Philippines

At the close of the Mass the priest splashed holy water over the photograph and then a more intimate group of a dozen or so stayed on to share stories of their brother Gene. Convenor of the morning, Remy Guillena noted that Gene's wish was to be cremated, "so he is now present to us in the wider cosmos." Malou Lauzon Manrique talked of Gene and Dorothy's active involvement in the Philippines, particularly in Mindanao, seeking justice for the poor, the disappeared, and for women. She recalled her initial meetings with Gene, remembering with surprise how such a big white American contained so much gentleness.

Annette Ferrer read a poem dictated to her over the phone by her father Tony Ferrer, who had suffered a stroke and could not come.

Manny Lahoz told of how Dorothy and Gene carried the energy they imbibed in the Philippines to Chicago, where they established SYNAPSES. There, they developed a quick response network that alerted people to disappearances in the Philippines, and then exerted pressure on government, military, and police authorities.

Rey Lopez, now of Christian Peacemaker Team—Philippines spoke of learning the techniques of creative nonviolence from Gene during his Chicago

March 15, 2009

days, He spoke of his relationship to Gene as that of "pastor to Bishop, and now my bishop is gone." He recalled Gene as a courageous and "cool" guy, ready to face the Tonton Macoute of Haiti with his smile. He had expected to see Gene in a few days, in Thailand.

Girlie Villariba, who led the procession at the offering at Mass, spoke of the recent healing Body Talk sessions and how prescient the word Synapses (Gene and Dorothy's solidarity organization in Chicago) was to what the group is doing now. She also talked of the connections activists made during martial law, and how Dorothy and Gene through Synapses nurtured the women's groups that have now come into full play.

Throughout the morning people recalled Gene and Dorothy's constant smiles, their "vivaciousness and living life fully."

Donald Goertzen spoke of first becoming acquainted with Gene and Dorothy in the 1970s when he re-typed and edited their monthly "Filipino Newsletter" which was distributed to several hundred people on their pre-internet mail list. This, and later meetings with them in Chicago led to his life-long involvement with the Philippines. He spoke of Gene's integrity and constancy, "you didn't have to be in touch with Gene on a regular basis to know what he was doing, he'd be organizing a training, agitating for justice, working for peace among people."

Remy Guillena, who sacrificed office work that day to emcee the sharing, recalled with emotion Gene's working days with the Mindanao Sulu Pastoral Conference staff in the late 70s. She recalled Gene's many travels through Mindanao and his passion for the workers and the marginalized he had listened to.

In closing, Len Abesamis thanked the "family" of Gene and Dorothy for showing up en masse. She noted that the event had been organized in less than 48 hours. She related her recent telephone call with Dorothy and recounted Gene's last moments in this life, enjoying the first warm day in Ontario, out enjoying nature he loved, on his motorbike. She said events had conspired, such that they show clearly that that was how it was meant to be, after Gene had lived a full and fulfilled life.

Following a rousing "Mabuhay" to Gene, his friends reconvened in the rectory of Bahay Ugnayan for merienda, more stories, and the exchange of email addresses and cell phone numbers as a newly-reconnected barkada.

Friends included Remy Rikken, Ching Gerlock, Sr. Marion Chipeco, RGS, Sr. Celine, RGS, Liza Almojuela, Godio and Nita Salazar, Salome Tibar, Manny and Angge Lahoz, Pangging Santos, Remy Guillena, Malou Manrique, Don Goertzen, Chito Generoso, Ditsi Carolino, Sr Sonia Punzalan, Ching Daclan, Venerando, Rey Lopez, Annette Ferrer, and Len Abesamis. It was a beautiful moment of sharing joy and sorrow, but Gene's adopted family felt he was now in a very good place, a much better place!

Memorials later in March 2010 were also held elsewhere in the Philippines: in Davao City, organized by Chic Ramoso, Helen Gaspar, Nonoy Rodriguez and Luz Rodriguez; in Olongapo, Zambales, organized by Alan Along and the Alliance for Bases Clean-up.

CHRONOLOGY

Mervin Eugene Stoltzfus
February 1, 1940—March 10, 2010

February 1, 1940: Born in Aurora, Ohio, the youngest of seven children. Parents, Orpha Beechy and Elmer Stoltzfus, had a dairy farm and gave leadership at the Plainview Mennonite Church. His father was pastor, and later, bishop.

1958: Graduated from Eastern Mennonite High School in Harrisonburg, Virginia and then attended Eastern Mennonite College for two years.

1962: Graduated from Goshen Mennonite College, Goshen, Indiana. Registered for the draft as a conscientious objector to war. He also took two years of seminary training in Goshen.

1963-67: Worked with International Voluntary Services in Vietnam until he resigned with other IVS volunteers in protest against the war.

1968-72: Washington, DC. Lobbied against the war and worked with the Indo-China Mobile Education Project.

1970: Graduated from American University with a Master's degree in Asian/ Southeast Asian Studies.

Fall 1972: Attended Associated Mennonite Biblical Seminaries in Elkhart Indiana to complete his Master of Divinity Degree in 1973.

1973-76: Director of Mennonite Voluntary Services for the General Conference of Mennonites in Newton, Kansas with a view to engaging with the domestic social justice needs of that day.

April, 1975: Marriage to Dorothy Friesen at the Sermon on the Mount Chapel at Associated Mennonite Biblical Seminaries, Elkhart Indiana.

1976-1979: Gene and Dorothy were co-directors of the Mennonite Central Committee program in the Philippines.

1979-80: On the road in Canada and the United States talking in schools, churches, to community and solidarity groups about the Philippines.

1981-1986: Chicago. Director of the Urban Life Center which provided students from midwestern colleges and universities a semester of direct engagement with urban resources realities, and issues.

1986-88: Chicago. Work with Synapses, a grass roots international peace, justice, and spirituality organization to connect people in the United States with people around world; with CUANES-Philippines, a human rights organization; and briefly at the national American Friends Service Committee in Philadelphia, Pennsylvania.

1988-2004: Founding Director of the Christian Peacemaker Teams (CPT), Chicago.

2004-2010: Retirement in Fort Frances, Ontario, with international speaking engagements in Europe and Japan, and peace actions, speeches and campaigns in the United States and Canada.

Boots

(In memory of Gene Stoltzfus, 1940-2010)

Orphaned at the roadside
beside the motor-assisted bicycle,
hat gone AWOL in a breeze
before the keening ambulance arrived,
departed with the uncomplaining
body. Plaid shirt, jeans
and on the bootless feet, grey socks.

The wind that day was not an omen,
just a gentle teasing. Nothing
to make the heart fail.
Yet body and bike collapsed
and fell
thudding on hard ground.

Where did the white-haired, bearded rider
think he was going when he laced up
his well-worn leather boots meant for walking?
Why was the destination altered mid-trip
as though he'd changed his mind?

The mode of travel too was changed,
as if he was given wings
swifter than a motorized bike,
swifter than shod feet.

While the rest of us sang together:
Guide my feet while I run this race...
and we are marching in the light of God,

Dorothy picked those worn boots up,
held them high, marched them through the air.
Laughter filled the sanctuary
and we cried, clapped our hands,
our bodies swayed. We couldn't stop
our feet from tapping time.

— *Sarah Klassen*
Winnipeg, Manitoba

THE EDITORS

Dorothy Friesen graduated from the Mennonite Biblical Seminary in Elkhart, Indiana, with a Master's degree in Peace Studies. She is the author of *Critical Choices: A Journey with the Filipino People* and a romance novel entitled *Stormy Ties*. She is a holistic health care practitioner with the International BodyTalk System Association.

Marilen Abesamis received her Master's degree in Women and Development at the Institute for Social Studies in The Hague. She is a teacher at an all-women's college and a promoter of BodyTalk in the Philippines.

To order copies of this publication visit:

www.createspaceforpeace.info
www.trimarkpress.com

Join us at the following sites:

www.createspaceforpeace.info
www.facebook.com/spaceforpeace
Twitter:@space4peace
www.peaceprobe.wordpress.com